My Dog Can Preach

40 Lessons of God's Love Unleashed

ROXANNE WORSHAM

ISBN 978-1-7364370-0-1 (Paperback)
ISBN 978-1-7364370-1-8 (Hardcover)
ISBN 978-1-7364370-2-5 (eBook)

Printed in the United States of America

DEDICATION

This book is dedicated in loving memory of my beloved mother, Virginia Schneider, who encouraged me to write it, and in memory of my sweet dog, Scout, who was the inspiration for it.

CONTENTS

Foreword

BY VICTORIA OSTEEN

As Christians, we believe that God created the Universe. He created the Earth, the sky, the oceans and every animal that exists. It should stand to reason then, if God created everything, we should be able to see Him in everything. The oceans and the mountains should prove that He exists and every living creature should testify as to who He is. *My Dog Can Preach*, written by my dear friend, Roxanne Worsham, illustrates this point in ways that are both insightful and understandable.

Many years ago, Roxanne brought her new puppy, Scout, over to our house. Joel and I, along with our children, fell in love with the little pup, and pretty soon our children wanted to get one just like him. So, we went out and did just that. We brought our female puppy home and it didn't take long for her to become part of our family.

As typical dog owners, we set out to teach her all the

things we wanted her to know: how to come when called, shake hands, roll over, and sit on command. The truth is, sometimes we can be so preoccupied with teaching lessons to our dogs that we may not realize the fact that they can teach us a few lessons as well. This is an observation that does not escape Roxanne's attention and one which she cleverly fashions into a series of short, relatable anecdotes that help us appreciate and strengthen our relationship with God and with each other.

When Roxanne told me about the idea for *My Dog Can Preach*, I was inspired but, quite frankly, not surprised. You see, Roxanne is not only a spiritual person with a deep and abiding faith in Jesus, but she is an intelligent and discerning woman who sees things in a unique way. When Roxanne looks at Scout, she doesn't just see a dog, she sees a creature fashioned by God. While her adorable puppy may not be created in God's image, he is nonetheless a living thing created by the One who created all living things.

In Roxanne's view, God didn't just place Scout in her home for mere companionship and entertainment, but for a greater purpose as well. Through Scout, Roxanne learned and shares with us the love of God, His purpose for our lives, and a myriad of lessons on how to not only live a more joyous and fulfilling life, but to be a blessing to everyone around us.

As you enjoy *My Dog Can Preach*, it is my hope that it will inspire you to discover and appreciate the many ways that God makes Himself known in your own life.

Introduction

*But ask the animals, and they will teach you, or the
birds in the sky, and they will tell you; or speak to the
earth, and it will teach you, or let the fish in the sea
inform you. Which of all these does not know that the
hand of the Lord has done this? In His hand is the life
of every creature and the breath of all mankind.*

JOB 12:7-10

God speaks to our hearts through many different avenues:
His written Word, the spoken word, and even through the
lyrics of songs. He also speaks to us through creation. For
some, the Lord may use a rainbow to remind them of His
promises. For others, they feel the Lord's presence near a
lake, the ocean, a mountain, or a still meadow. All the earth
declares the glory of God, meaning that all the earth shows
the manifestation of God's presence, and as we see in the
above scripture, He even uses animals. When my friend sees
a redbird, she is aware that God is speaking to her heart. We
see in scripture that God used a talking donkey, and for me,
He very often uses my two dogs.

How amazing is it that we have people in our lives who
help us get closer to God. Isn't it delightful that the Lord can
use a dog, or any pet, for the same purpose? Now, if you are
like me, you love your pet like a family member—and probably your favorite family member. Why? Well, several things

come to my mind but first of all, my dogs never tell me "no." They let me do whatever I want, whenever I want. They love me unconditionally, and they are always happy to see me. No, actually they are *thrilled* to see me!

Each. And. Every. Time.

Anyone who has owned a dog knows that their unconditional love and acceptance is one of their most prominent characteristics. But there is so much more we can learn from our four-legged fur babies. By studying creation, we learn about the Creator.

Between the covers of this book are stories of my dog Scout and his brother Arrow. These are stories of how God used two very unlikely candidates to teach me His simple truths, biblical principles, and to remind me how valuable and loved I am. My purpose in sharing these treasured moments with you is to help you become fully aware that God is alive and active in your life even in the seemingly ordinary things. He wants to reveal His love to you in new ways and His creation tells the story of His character, faithfulness, and love. Yes, all of creation speaks for goodness sake! The very rocks will testify if need be!

My prayer for you is that you learn the breadth, height, and depth of Jesus' love for you. As you read these pages, I hope you begin to see God in your everyday life as well and you too will agree that my dog can preach. I am sure yours can too!

Enjoy!

Roxanne

You Are Chosen

When we were searching for the perfect dog to join our family, we did a lot of research. We knew we wanted a friendly dog. We wanted a dog that didn't shed, one that was hypoallergenic, and we also wanted a breed that was known for being loving and sweet. Once we narrowed it down to breeds that had everything on our checklist, we were confident that a Shih Tzu was the best choice for us!

Next, we had to read and learn about breeders and find the one who was the most reputable. Once we found the right breeder, we then had to choose just the right pup from the litter. This was the most difficult of all the decisions as each puppy was absolutely precious. I'll never forget the day we made our choice. My husband, Mills, and I were selecting a puppy to give to our young son, Rob, as a surprise for Christmas. We were so excited and full of joy when we arrived at the breeder's home and went inside to see the new litter. The pups were about eight weeks old and so innocently and curiously exploring their new world, crawling all over each other, and figuring out their rank in the pack. We watched them interact with one another and observed how different their little personalities were. Some were bold and playful while others were reserved and more laid back.

When the breeder let them out of their cage to meet us, they all came running toward us, melting our hearts! We spent quite a bit of time holding and getting to know each pup before we chose the one that we thought would be the perfect fit for our family. That is the day we chose Scout, a 1.5 lb. jet black, bright-eyed little boy, who became the furry darling of our family.

What would it mean for Scout to be chosen by the Worsham Family? It meant that he would be loved and provided for at all times. It meant that we would feed him and take care of his health. We would make sure he was well-groomed and clean and that he would always have a home with us.

Even as Scout was chosen, did you know that you are chosen too? Yes! God looked over all His creation, and He chose you to love and care for in ways far beyond what you could ever realize. The Bible says that before He formed you in your mother's womb, God knew you. He chose you because He wants you to know how valuable you are and how deeply and uniquely loved you are. Stop and think about that for a moment. The Creator of the Universe made you and chose you to call His own.

Do you remember in grade school when the kids would choose teams for a game such as kickball during recess? There were always one or two students who were left out. It was so nerve-racking for everyone waiting to hear their name called, and it was so sad to see the faces of those who didn't get chosen. Another similar childhood memory was in gym class when we were learning to square dance. All the boys would line up on one side of the gymnasium and all the girls lined up on the other. Then the physical education teacher would tell the boys to go choose a girl. The boys ran across the gym to choose their square-dancing partner. Thankfully I always got picked, but my heart broke for the few girls who were left. But here's the Good News! Unlike choosing a new pet, or picking teams for kickball, or choosing a square dance partner, God will NEVER leave you out. You are always chosen by Him!

For you are a people holy to the LORD your God. Out of all the peoples on the face of the earth, the LORD has chosen you to be His treasured possession.

DEUTERONOMY 14:2

I don't know about you, friend, but knowing that the Lord chose me touches my heart. It also makes me very curious. Why would God choose me? Who am I that He would be mindful of me and even consider me?

Jesus says, "You did not choose me, but I chose you and appointed you so that you might go and bear fruit—fruit that will last—and so that whatever you ask in My name, the Father will give you" (John 15:16). Why did God choose you? He chose you because of His great love and mercy. He chose you because it pleased Him. The Bible says that He chose you to showcase His character and display His glory. God chose you to join Him in the work that He prepared in advance for you to do. He has a divine plan, and you are part of it. You are chosen because you are loved. I told you that we chose our dog, and while we chose him first, one thing I discovered is that our dog chose us as well. How do I know that? There are lots of other pet owners we walk by each day on our afternoon strolls. Scout does not leave me and go to one of them. He stays with me. He walks beside me. He listens to my voice. He chooses me just as I chose him. I know the Lord chose me for Himself, but I also chose Him for myself. The Lord wants to make it plain and clear that before we ever chose Him, He had already chosen us; but we have to choose Him every day in return. We have to choose to stay close to Him and follow His leading. We have to choose to listen to His voice.

Today, tune out the distractions of the world. Meditate on this truth that you are chosen and let it instill value into your heart. Receive His love, grace, and power in every area of your life as you choose Him in return.

. . . .

Dear Heavenly Father, thank You so much for choosing me, and in return I choose You too! I always want to stay close to You and never leave Your side. Thank You for displaying Your love and truth in creation and in the simple things of life. I don't always understand why You chose me as Your own, but I am so grateful and so humbled. I commit everything I am to You. In Jesus' name I pray, amen.

Time to Paws...

Today and every day, I will remember that I am chosen by God, my Heavenly Father. I will tell others that they are chosen as well.

_____

_____

_____

_____

_____

_____

_____

_____

_____

_____

_____

_____

_____

_____

A Great Gift

After we chose Scout, we had to wait a few more weeks before he could come home with us. But let me tell you, it was love at first sight! He was the cutest puppy in the litter. His soft fur was so thick, curly, and dark that you could barely see his big brown eyes. We couldn't wait to surprise our son Rob, who was in the third grade at the time, on Christmas morning with his very first puppy!

After we were able to pick Scout up from the breeder, we took all the precautionary measures with the vet and gave him his first shots. Then we took him to my brother Fred's home to keep him a secret for a few days until Christmas. Several times a day, I would go over to Fred's apartment to see Scout and bond with him and let him know how wanted and loved he was. I also wanted to remind my sweet brother that this was a gift for his nephew and not to get too attached! When Fred started calling him "Bear," I knew I was in trouble! Christmas morning finally arrived. Mills and I were so excited and could not wait to see the joy on our son's face. We woke up early and took the new puppy into Rob's bedroom and placed him on the bed next to our sleeping son. The little puppy woke Rob up with kisses all over his face. I cannot adequately express the joy and elation that was on our son's face when he saw his dog. It was love at first sight for all of us, and a new joy came into all our lives that day. The tiny little ball of soft fur with his big brown eyes made a home in our family and a home in our hearts.

As great as that Christmas morning was with this special gift of a furry life, it truly pales in comparison to the Greatest Gift we all were given one morning in a stable in Bethlehem. This Gift was not just a gift for a little boy, but He is the Gift to all mankind, and His name is Jesus. In all of God's wisdom, He chose to introduce the King of all kings to the world in the form of a baby. How amazing and yet so odd, a baby King! I've thought about that very act a lot over the years and realized how genius it was. Not that God needs my approval or opinion but ponder it with me for a moment.

A baby is so innocent, so approachable. No one is ever threatened by a baby! We all want to get near the innocence and purity of a baby, and I believe that is exactly what God intended. He wants us all to draw near to His Son, Jesus. He wants us to embrace Jesus and believe in Him so that we can receive the gift of eternal life with Him.

When Scout was still a young puppy, I would take him with me to pick up Rob from school. Rob was always so proud to share his precious pup with all his friends at school. His classmates would get so excited to see Scout, to pet him, and "*oooh* and *ahhh*" over him. One of Rob's classmates liked Scout so much that he and his family decided to get a dog just like him. When you have a gift that is so great, you want to share it with the world. You wish that everyone could have the same blessing that you have.

That is the way I feel about the best gift that I know and have in my heart. I want to share Jesus with the world, and I especially want to share Him with you. He is my best friend who sticks closer than a brother. Not only is He the One who saved me and forgave me of all my sins, but He is the Lord of my life. He sits on the throne of my heart. He is always near to hear every single conversation. He wipes away the tears from my eyes. He mends my broken heart, He lifts me when I am sad, and He cheers me on as I run this race of life.

For God so loved the world that He gave His one and only Son, that whoever believes in Him shall not perish but have eternal life.

JOHN 3:16

Of all the gifts we could ever be given, there is not a greater gift to all humanity than the gift of Jesus the Christ, our Messiah. The Bible says anyone who calls on the name of the Lord shall be saved. I hope and pray you have opened and received Jesus as your very own. He is the Savior for mankind and the lover of your souls. Jesus came to us to bring Heaven to earth and to show us a better way, the way back to our Heavenly Father. If you have not asked Jesus into your heart to be the Lord of your life, I would like to invite you to do so. Please turn to page 238 and allow me the honor to lead you in a simple prayer. The Bible says that if you would just believe in your heart and confess with your mouth as you call upon the name of Jesus, you will be saved.

· ·

Dear Heavenly Father, Thank You for loving me. Thank You for giving me the greatest gift I could ever receive, Your Son Jesus. I believe that He died on the cross for my sins and rose again to live forever. I believe, and receive, that all my sins are forgiven, and You remember them no more. Jesus, please come into my heart and be my Lord and my Savior. I put You on the throne of my life. My faith and Your amazing grace have saved me. In Jesus' name I pray, amen.

Time to Paws...

Today I will tell someone about my decision to follow Jesus. I will begin to pray and talk to the Lord like I would my best friend. I will begin to read my Bible and ask the Lord to help me in every facet of my life.

_____

_____

_____

_____

_____

_____

_____

_____

_____

_____

_____

_____

I Will Never Leave You

Every morning as I leave my bedroom and walk down the hall, my little buddy, Scout, is right there leading the way. Scout is a precocious and charming, jet black, pure-bred Shih Tzu. He is so loyal and always right there with me. He proudly prances down the hall in front of me, wagging his tail, with a pep in each step.

One day I noticed that he kept glancing back at me to make sure that I was still following him. He would take a few steps and then look back at his momma. He would take a few more steps and cast yet another glance my way. This particular day Scout assumed that I was walking all the way down the hallway to my office as I had done so many times before; however, little did he know that I had a different plan and path for myself that morning. He passed by the opening into the den and kept walking toward my office. He kept thinking he was leading the way, but I wasn't really following him.

I turned to go into the den, and when Scout noticed, he stopped in his tracks, immediately turned around, and jumped in front of me again, taking his place as the leader.

He was determined to lead me and never leave me no matter where I decided to go. It was as if Scout was demonstrating to me exactly what I think the Lord speaks to me at times, "Roxanne, I will never leave you. No matter where you go, I will be there with you. I want to lead you. I prefer you go this way because it leads to a better life for you, the life I have prepared for you. Nonetheless, I will be by your side no matter what! If you go to the highest height, I will be there. If you go to the lowest of lows, you can never escape My love for you. You are My prized possession! I want to be with you."

The Lord says, "I will guide you along the best pathway for your life. I will advise you and watch over you."

PSALM 32:8 NLT

Isn't it so comforting to know that you have a friend who wants to guide you? Aren't you happy to know that God is walking beside you and leading you no matter where you go? Best of all, He will never leave you.

The LORD Himself goes before you and will be with you; He will never leave you nor forsake you. Do not be afraid; do not be discouraged.

DEUTERONOMY 31:8

We have a true friend in God who is always watching

over us, leading us, guiding us, and directing us. He has a path marked out for you and me, but I believe it is up to us to ask Him what that path is and then follow Him on it. Just as Scout leads me and desires that I follow him, God is leading each of us and desires that we follow Him.

Friend, I don't know where you are in your life right now. I don't know if you are close to God or far from Him. What I do know is that it is never too late to get on the right path with Him. He wants to lead you away from danger and onto a path that leads to life everlasting.

That's not to say that when you follow the path God has for you difficulties won't arise, but with the Lord close, you will be more able to navigate those trials and tribulations. One thing you can always be sure of is that God will never leave you abandoned or stranded. Once you belong to Him, He will be with you in every season and every situation.

This illustration of God never leaving me is the very first "sermon" my dog ever preached to me. I will never forget that moment when the Holy Spirit gave me this revelation. After that, I began to notice more and more biblical truths and principles displayed in the behavior and characteristics of my dog.

I was so taken aback as to why the Lord was using my pet to teach me, but isn't it just like God to use the simple things in life to confound the wise? I called my mom and told her what I observed, and she encouraged me to write everything down and told me that one day I might write a book! (It really is true...mothers know best!)

All throughout the Bible, the Lord used animals to help

His people. One time He caused a fish to have coins in its mouth that were used to pay taxes. Another time He caused a donkey to speak in human language. Jesus is called a lion, and He is also known as a lamb. I know that our Heavenly Father uses my dog often to speak His messages to me. As elementary and as strange as it may sound, it is true and the whole basis for which I can write this book. God is always speaking, but are we always listening? He is always leading us, will we follow Him?

. . . .

Dear Heavenly Father, thank You for Your promise to never leave me and that You will always be my guide. Thank You that You are always with me no matter where I go, and I am never alone. Please help me to see clearly the best path that You have planned for me, and help me to always follow You. I invite You to lead, and I commit to follow. Help me to stay close to You always. In Jesus' name I pray, amen.

Time to Paws...

Today I will be mindful that God is leading me and walking with me every step I take. I walk confidently knowing that He will never leave me.

_____

_____

_____

_____

_____

_____

_____

_____

_____

_____

_____

_____

_____

_____

The Dawn of a New Day

My morning routine varies slightly depending on which day of the week it is. It may begin with a cup of coffee and quiet time, or it may begin with me rushing to the shower to get ready for work because I hit the snooze button one too many times, or got lost in my social media feed. Regardless of the day of the week, there is always one constant, and I bet you can guess that is Scout.

Scout fits his name perfectly. First and foremost, he scouts me out every morning. When I open my eyes, he is always right there by the bed looking straight at me with his little fluffy tail wagging with delight. Like any good scout, he finds me wherever I am and then never lets me out of his sight. He follows me into the kitchen when I go to pour that first cup of coffee. He runs past me down the hall when I am heading to the shower. Sometimes he just sits in my bathroom and stares at me while I apply a fresh coat of paint to this face of mine. I often wonder why it is that our dogs like to stare at us so much. I wish I were truly as exciting as he believes that I am! I keep reminding him that he is the exciting one who looks so cute and does all the tricks. Even though Scout sits and looks at me with those huge dark eyes and long eyelashes, most of the time I am too hurried or too busy to give him any attention. In my mind, I know I'll have time later. When I am rushing to get out the door, I will walk right past him and pretty much ignore him. I am busy with things to do so I don't stop to acknowledge him as I should. On those busy mornings, I tend to be so focused on my day and my "to do" list that I barely glance at him or acknowledge his faithfulness, affection, and loyalty to me. I rush past his stare and don't consider the love he has for me at that moment.

One day it dawned on me, "I wonder if that is how God feels. I wonder if He feels neglected and overlooked." Every morning I awaken with new breath in my lungs. I am grateful for a new day, but do I stop to thank the One who gave it to me? All my little four-legged furry family member wants is a little attention and some love. How much more does God deserve our attention and love?

He gave us such a glorious life, a loving family, a roof over our head, a new day of blessings, and a myriad of other things, but do we take the time to consider His blessings and gifts in our lives? Do we acknowledge Him and express our gratefulness?

What would happen if we would just "paws" every morning and throughout the day to notice Him and thank Him? Wouldn't it be great if we greeted Him each morning with a "Thank You, God, for another day?" I wonder what our day would look like if we thought about the Lord before our feet even hit the floor, and we whispered a sincere, "Good Morning, Heavenly Father. I love You so much." Even before we pick up our phones, start scrolling through social media, reading texts, or responding to emails, what if we began our day giving thanks to the One who gave it to us?

What if we acknowledge that before our eyes open, His eyes are upon us? What if we ask the Lord to be with us throughout the day or... what if we got crazy and asked the Lord how we could participate with Him in whatever He had in mind to accomplish that day?

Whatever is good and perfect comes to us from God above, who created all heaven's lights. Unlike them, He never changes or casts shifting shadows. In His goodness He chose to make us His own children by giving us His true word. And we, out of all creation, became His choice possession.

JAMES 1:17-18 NLT

Just as our furry friends want our affection, time, and attention, I believe the Lord Himself would like our affection, time, and attention, too. The Bible says that He created us for His pleasure. We are His prized possession, His masterpiece! It pleased God to create you. It pleases Him even more to have a relationship with you. Any good and healthy relationship has to be two sided. A great relationship is full of monologue and dialogue. It needs to be "give and take" with both sides giving 100%. God, our Father, created every living thing. When He created the animals, He said it was good. But when He created you and me, He looked at us so lovingly and said it was very good! You, my friend, are a very good thing! You have so much potential inside of you that was placed there by your Creator God. Your Heavenly Father knew what you would need to accomplish and fulfill the great and rewarding life that He has for you. You are more than enough, God's very own masterpiece whom He loves and cherishes. Don't ever be in such a hurry that you miss the blessing of connecting with Him each day.

Dear Heavenly Father, thank You for the gift of each dawn of a new day. Thank You for waking me and watching over me. I choose to put You first and to be more mindful to focus on You and what You have in store for me. I will take time each day, and even set a reminder if needed, to think about You and thank You because You are worthy of all my praise. I love You, and thank You for loving me and creating me for Your glory. In Jesus' name I pray, amen.

Time to Paws...

Today I will be mindful that God is active in my life. I will give God thanks throughout the day for being so good to me. I will focus on being more intentional in my relationship with Jesus.

God's Gaze

Why is it that our dogs love to stare at us? I find that so funny and peculiar. It reminds me of a time when I was first married—I woke up one morning and my husband Mills was leaning over me, intently staring at me. His face was about six inches from mine when I opened my eyes. I was a little bit weirded out, and I asked him, "What in the world are you doing?"

He replied, "I was just looking at how beautiful you are and how peaceful you look." (Notice I said, "When I was first married.") Things have changed now. Ha ha. Actually, my husband is still that sweet to me. While my husband isn't staring at me all day long, quite often I catch my dog gazing in my direction, staring at me. When I am in the bathroom brushing my teeth or washing my face, he sits near watching me intently. If I am sitting in my favorite chair, he will position himself on the arm of the sofa adjacent from me so that he has a clear view of me and a perfect staring position. He will sit there for hours if I am watching a movie with my husband. He never tires of looking at me. I wish I were as great as he makes me feel. If I am in my office working, he lays on the floor near me. Now he doesn't lay right at my feet, mind you. He lays a few feet away so he can have his watchful eye upon me and every single thing I do. It is the most curious thing. Literally and figuratively, he positions himself to stare at me.

This staring business has always baffled me until I had a talk with my friend Joanna about it. She informed me that there is research that strongly suggests that a hormone called oxytocin is released when an owner and his pet gaze at one another.

This act of staring into your pet's eyes is joyous for them, calming for you, and builds trust between you both. Oxytocin is the bonding chemical. It is the same hormone that is released between a newborn and its mother. I remember just staring at my newborn son for hours studying every single line and feature. His image was embedded and ingrained so deeply within my heart that I could still see his every feature even when my eyes were closed.

The Bible teaches us that God has His watchful eye upon us. After reading the research that I mentioned above, it makes perfect sense to me. Of course, God would watch us. He loves us! He created us in His own image. We are His masterpiece!

The eyes of the LORD are toward the righteous and
His ears toward their cry.

PSALM 34:15 ESV

Behold, the eye of the LORD is on those who fear Him,
on those who hope in His steadfast love.

PSALM 33:18

Sometimes I marvel because God thought of everything! Why would the God of all the Universe be so concerned with me that He would watch my every move? Doesn't God have bigger things to deal with? Friend, let me tell you that you are God's biggest deal! He calls you the apple of His eye because He loves you so very much. You are His precious child.

When you are in love with someone, you do gaze in their direction and give them your full attention. The relationship we have with the Father through His Son Jesus is similar. The Bible says that God's eyes run to and fro looking at those whose hearts are committed to Him. God wants to strengthen us with His watchful eye upon us. He wants to keep His watchful eye upon us because He loves us so very much.

For the eyes of the LORD range throughout the
earth to strengthen those whose hearts are fully
committed to Him...

2 CHRONICLES 16:9a

As much as your dog loves to stare at you because he loves you so much, how much more does your Heavenly Father want to set His gaze upon you? Not one little sparrow falls to the ground that Father God is not fully aware of in the moment of its fall. If He cares that much for a little birdie, think for a moment how much He cares for you, His very own son or daughter. Don't you find such comfort knowing that the watchful eye of a loving Father is upon you? Now when I see my dog gazing at me with such love, it reminds me that my Heavenly Father is watching over me with love and kindness.

For His eyes are upon the ways of a man,
and He sees all his steps.

JOB 34:21 ESV

. . . .

Dear Heavenly Father, thank You for always watching over me and taking care of me. It is so humbling and comforting to know that You have Your watchful eye upon me. I pray that I may gaze more often and intently in Your direction in return, strengthening my faith and securing my hope. I love You, Lord, and want to love You more. In Jesus' name I pray, amen.

Time to Paws...

Today I will remember that God is watching over me and sees everything. I will be mindful that God has His loving eye upon me, and nothing escapes Him.

_____

_____

_____

_____

_____

_____

_____

_____

_____

_____

_____

_____

6

The Best Hugs

I love it so very much when I hold my sweet Scout and he rests his head on me. It's as if he is giving me a hug. When this happens, I feel an exchange of love taking place. It is such a comfortable feeling for me to know that he is demonstrating his love because he trusts me, and he is most comfortable with me. It is the highest compliment he can give to me. I could hold him like that forever and we both feel so content.

I remember all the snuggles with my newborn son and how precious that time was. The bonding, the love, the peaceful feeling with each embrace, are some of my fondest memories. I would hold Rob for hours and pat his little back. One sweet day, I felt his tiny hand begin to pat me on the shoulder in return and it absolutely melted my heart. Giving love and hugs came naturally to him.

I will never forget a time when Rob was only six months old. A very dear friend of mine had lost four of her five children in a horrific car accident, and we attended their funeral service. Mills and I were there with baby Rob at the graveside service. After the service, the father of the children asked if he could hold Rob. Rob went right to him and touched the dad's face with his precious little hands. Then he rested his head on the man's shoulder to comfort him and love him. I was so taken aback, wondering how this tiny baby knew that this dad needed a hug. The image and memory are forever etched in my head and emblazoned upon my heart.

We can never underestimate the power in a touch or an embrace. I am so well known for my very heartfelt hugs that my friends have said I have a "hug ministry." If you are going to hug me, I want one that actually means something and one that I can feel, so I tend to hug others by the same guidelines. One can sense the authenticity of a hug and the feeling of a safe place to rest that comes with it.

There is very well-known research that speaks to the importance and value of touching and hugging. A hug is a tangible act of love that one can use to express gratitude, sympathy, kindness, care, and deep emotion. Hugs promote emotional attachment in our relationships. It is a universal language all its own.

Sometimes we aren't able to physically hug others, but there is something just as comforting and powerful, and those are words of encouragement, kindness, and love that we can give at just the right time to another person when we can't be there in person. I think that is how God hugs us. We may not be able to wrap our arms around Him physically at this time, but His empowering truth is like a warm embrace to our souls. I also believe He hugs us through other people who act on His behalf in our time of need. The "hugs" we receive from Jesus spur us on to hug others by meeting their needs as well.

I will never forget one time when a "friend" said something incredibly hurtful to me. My heart literally ached and I was crushed to the core. I was in my bedroom crying, praying, and wondering what in the world just happened. How could anyone deliberately hurt someone in that way? About thirty minutes later, my dear friend Ricky, an executive chef at a popular restaurant, sent me a text out of the blue during the height of his lunch rush. His words were completely unexpected, yet so kind and encouraging and could not have come at a more perfect time.

I asked him about it a few days later and he said, "Roxanne, I was in the kitchen cooking and so busy. The Lord brought you to my mind and prompted me to message you and tell you how special you are. I tried to put it off until later, but the feeling would not leave me. I tried to keep working but couldn't. I knew I had to send the message right then so I stopped everything and got my phone to text you."

Now that is what a hug from God looks like! A God hug is the best hug because it isn't temporary; it brings lasting comfort and healing to our inner most beings. The compassion of Jesus never fails and is available to every single person.

God loves to hug His children and He does it in so many ways—whether through the words of a friend, the snuggles of a newborn, or through a little fur ball sprawled across your lap. Receive His loving embrace and let it restore you today.

Praise be to the God and Father of our Lord Jesus Christ, the Father of compassion and the God of all comfort, who comforts us in all our troubles, so that we can comfort those in any trouble with the comfort we ourselves receive from God.

2 CORINTHIANS 1:3-4

. . . .

Dear Heavenly Father, thank You for being so close and for caring about the things that concern me. Thank You for the gift of Your embrace that heals and restores me. Help me feel Your loving arms around me and teach me how I can hug others on Your behalf with my words, my actions, my deeds, my generosity, and my kindness. In Jesus' name I pray, amen.

Time to Paws...

Today I will be on the lookout for others who need a hug from God. When I give it to them, I will be sure and tell them that it is from their Heavenly Father who loves them so very much.

_____

_____

_____

_____

_____

_____

_____

_____

_____

_____

_____

_____

_____

_____

_____

How Much is That Doggie in the Window?

As a young girl, one of my very favorite songs to sing with my siblings was, you guessed it, "How Much is that Doggie in the Window?" Now, I am one of eleven children, right in the middle of six girls and five boys. When my siblings and I would sing that lighthearted childhood song, it was my duty to bark at the appropriate time, "ruff, ruff!" Even five decades later, a smile comes across my face as I recall that fond memory. (If you buy the audible book, I am almost certain that I will sing it for you!)

Naturally, when we bought Scout from the breeder, that song was rolling through my head; and I finally got my answer. That "doggie in the window" wasn't cheap! However, I never once considered the cost because he was the dog we wanted. I know others who spent way more than we did for their beloved fur babies. Not to mention, when a dog gets hurt or sick, you can spend thousands of dollars to give him the medical attention that he needs. For us, we couldn't count the cost because love knows no limits. When it comes to love, you can't put a price tag on it.

So much greater than the price of caring for our beloved pets is the price that was placed on you. God spared no expense to redeem you and call you His own. Jesus paid the ultimate price and ransom for you. He paid with His very own life.

For you are bought with a price: therefore glorify God in your body, and in your spirit, which are God's.

I CORINTHIANS 6:20 KJV

One of my favorite stories in the Bible is a parable found in Matthew. It speaks of a man finding a pearl of great price. The man knew it was an incredible treasure and he wanted to have it. Although he had vast wealth, he sold all that he had to be able to purchase that one pearl. He knew that he had found something precious and invaluable. Scripture compares the pearl to the Kingdom of God. It is a great treasure that is worth giving up everything we have to obtain it.

That is also how God feels about you! You are precious and priceless to Him. He loves you so much and wants a personal relationship with you. The book of Romans tells us that sin is what separates us from a Holy God. Sin holds us captive, but Jesus paid our ransom. Jesus agreed with His Father that you are worth it, and He paid the supreme price to wash away your sin and bring you close to Him. He bought you with His redeeming, forgiving, and atoning blood. He laid down His life so that you and I could gain ours. The Bible says that Jesus endured the pain, agony, shame, and humiliation of the cross with joy. Why joy? It was because Jesus was thinking of you during all of that, my friend. He loves you so much that He laid down His life with joy because He knew He would have you as His beloved child. When it comes to love, even when the stakes are so high, Jesus knows you are worth it.

What do we do with information like this? Surely a sacrifice of such love demands a response. My loving advice is to do what the man who found the pearl did. Recognize the treasure that you have. Make living for Jesus your greatest priority. Seek Him first in all that you do. Get to know Jesus through His Word. Talk to Him in prayer. Learn about Him and from Him. Whether it costs you time, resources, friends, or anything else, know that He is worth it. Just as He spared no expense for you, determine today to spare no expense for Him.

. . . .

Dear Heavenly Father, what a privilege it is to be loved by You! Thank You for pursuing me and redeeming me through the blood of Your Son Jesus. I'm so grateful that You paid the ultimate price so that I can live for all eternity with You. Today, I present all of my life to You and will use it to bring You glory and honor as a way to show my gratitude for all that You have done for me. I love You, Lord, and I will let nothing stand in the way of my relationship with You. In Jesus' name I pray, amen.

Time to Paws...

Today I will remember how valuable I am because I am so loved. I will be sure to tell others how valuable they are and the price Jesus paid for them because He loves them so much.

_____

_____

_____

_____

_____

_____

_____

_____

_____

_____

_____

_____

He Hears You

By great design, dogs can hear far better than humans. My pooch can hear things that I can't hear at all. I can whisper his name ever so faintly, and his little ears perk up as he looks straight at me, letting me know I have his full attention. When Mills drives into the driveway, I usually don't hear him until the car door closes. My dog perks up way before that and alerts me that daddy is home.

I remember when my son was an infant, I was so keenly aware of every little whimper. It was as if I had "super mom" hearing during that season. Not only that, but I could also tell by his different cries whether he was hungry, if he was tired, or needed changing. My ears were so sensitive to his every need and want. With each sound my child made, I was all ears just waiting to see how I could help him with whatever it was that he needed.

It is truly amazing how our sense of hearing is heightened when we tune in. I remember a time back in college when I was a Resident Assistant who helped look out for the girls that were assigned to me on my floor. One year, I had an incoming freshman who was legally blind, named Angie. I will never forget Angie as long as I live because I learned so much from her. I would often walk her down to the cafeteria and help her with her tray. She would hold the back of my arm ever so lightly. As we made our way through the cafeteria line, I would tell her what the food choices were for the day, and she would make her selections. I would sit and eat with her so I could learn from her. She was very bright and so fun to be around. She would often read to me from her big braille books.

A couple of years after I earned my undergraduate degree in education, I found myself back on that college campus as a graduate student. One day, to my utter delight, I saw Angie across campus. I yelled her name as loud as I could to get her attention. She stopped in her tracks as I ran toward her. She turned around and said, "Roxanne! Is that you?!" I almost cried because I was so happy to see her. I was so honored that she remembered me. She even recognized the sound of my voice all those years later. Do you know that God recognizes your voice too? Out of over 7,800,000,000 of His children who reside on this planet, the Lord can distinguish your voice calling on His name. He is attentive to your every cry and He delights in meeting your needs.

I love the LORD, for He heard my voice; He heard my cry for mercy. Because He turned his ear to me, I will call on Him as long as I live.

PSALM 116:1-2

If God designed and created dogs to hear 1,000 times better than humans, can you even imagine what the Lord's hearing must be like in comparison? He has multiple requests and cries that He tends to at any given moment. What a comforting and amazing thought.

El Shama, the God who hears, hears your voice and knows when you are calling out to Him. Not only that, He turns His ear toward you to hear every request. Not one voice is more precious to Him than yours. When you cry out to your Heavenly Father, He stops what He is doing to listen. He will send ten thousand angels to assist you because that is how much He loves you.

I constantly marvel that the Lord uses something as keen as my dog's hearing to remind me of who He is and how much He loves me. I love knowing that God is attentive to my voice and my pleas. He never grows tired of hearing your calls to rescue you either. He loves hearing your voice when you thank Him for all that He does for you. He especially loves to hear you tell Him how much you love Him and how thankful you are for Jesus.

Always remember, before you even utter a sound, He already knows your request. He longs to connect with you, and it blesses Him to meet every one of your needs. He is a great and loving Father. You are His precious child, and He always hears you!

Dear Heavenly Father, I can't even begin to thank You enough for hearing every single prayer I pray and for giving me Your full attention. I love You so much and I am so thankful that You love me with Your everlasting love. As You always turn Your ear to me, I will turn my heart fully toward You. In Jesus' name I pray, amen.

Time to Paws...

Today I will focus on the fact that every time I cry out to God, He hears me and is attentive to my needs and desires. As I hear familiar voices, I will be reminded that my voice is very familiar to my loving Heavenly Father.

_____

_____

_____

_____

_____

_____

_____

_____

_____

_____

_____

_____

_____

_____

The Power of Praise

Loud barking is a daily occurrence in my home. I find it so strange that such a little critter can make such a thunderous noise. When someone passes by my home, whether it be a neighbor walking down the sidewalk, the mailman delivering the day's bills, or the trash men gathering the refuse of the week, my little dog goes into full protection mode. He begins to bark so loudly and rapidly that my heart skips a beat, and it can truly get on my nerves! He has no regard for what I'm doing. He does not care one iota that I may be on a phone call, in the middle of a Zoom meeting, or recording a Facebook live. He barks and barks and barks and lets the trespasser know that he is too close for comfort. I immediately tell Scout to "hush" and sometimes raise my voice to try to get him to be quiet to no avail.

One day I tried a different approach. I would like to tell you that I changed my approach because I possess a very calm, collected demeanor, but that is just not the truth. The reason I tried this new tactic was because I was in the middle of a live video teaching and had an online audience who could hear my dog's ruckus; and of course, they could hear my response to it. In front of my audience, I began to praise my dog for taking care of us and being our great defender. Much to my surprise, the barking stopped immediately! I was not only shocked, but I looked like a genius to my online audience and almost fell out of my chair!

I went on to tell him how thankful I was that he was so brave and put our safety over his own. Then, as if I was writing a most amazing script, he came right over to me without a sound and curled up on the floor next to me and stayed with me. Apparently, he loved the gentleness in my voice and the affirmation, adoration, and accolades! It was the sweetest thing ever to witness. Try this with your dog; it is truly amazing! I even double-dog-dare to say, try it with your children and husband to see how the mood and atmosphere changes!

A gentle answer turns away wrath, but a harsh
word stirs up anger. The tongue of the wise adorns
knowledge, but the mouth of the fool gushes folly.
The eyes of the LORD are everywhere, keeping watch
on the wicked and the good. The soothing tongue is a
tree of life, but a perverse tongue crushes the spirit.

PROVERBS 15:1-4

Everyone loves to be praised and commended for a job well done. Like my dog, we all love kind words of affirmation and respond favorably to them. For some people, like me, "words of affirmation" is their favorite love language. This is the primary way I show love and receive love.

Did you know that God loves your praises as well? In fact, scripture says He inhabits them. To inhabit means to be right there occupying the space and territory. If Scout is drawn to me when I build him up, how much more does God show up on the scene when we honor and praise Him? Isn't it something to know that when we begin to open our mouths and say, "Thank You, Lord, for another day," that He is right there listening to us? When we thank Jesus for all that He has done, the One who sits enthroned is listening to our affirming and adoring words of gratitude and thanks. Every single time I begin to praise the One who is worthy of all praise, He is right there with me.

The Bible says we should enter God's presence with praise and thanksgiving. Who doesn't want to be in the presence of God? I know I sure do! What I marvel at is that God wants to be in *our* presence, too. He loves to be with us and commune with us, His precious sons and daughters. He delights in our praise as we delight in Him.

I have so much for which I am thankful, and I let the Lord know how grateful I am for His many blessings. Not only am I thankful for my dogs, but I thank Him for my husband, my son, my family, my friends, my church, my job, and a myriad of other things.

Recently, I began thanking Jesus for things that I am not aware of and things I can't see. For example, I thank Him for dreams coming to pass and blessings that He has laid up in store for me. I also thank Him for the things He protected me from.

Just like praising my dog immediately changed the atmosphere and his response, I believe an attitude of praise immediately changes me. When I begin to focus on all God has done for me, it ignites my heart and gets me going in the right direction again. We praise Jesus because He's worthy!

The next time you praise your dog for being so precious, or for bringing you his favorite toy, why don't you stop and begin to praise God for being so good to you? Shower the God of all Creation with your affection and adoration. You can be sure that He will be right there with you when you do!

. . . .

Dear Heavenly Father, thank You for loving me and for always being with me. Today I receive Your truth into my heart that a gentle word can change the atmosphere in my home. I want others to respond to my kindness and gentleness. Please help me to always be mindful of my tone and my words. In Jesus' name I pray, amen.

Time to Paws...

Today I will focus on praising God for the big things and the little things. When I hear someone say something nice to me, and when I see my dog responding to my words of affirmation, it will remind me to open my mouth and thank God for His goodness and faithfulness in my life.

_____

_____

_____

_____

_____

_____

_____

_____

_____

_____

_____

_____

_____

Without Saying a Word

Just like humans, dogs use their body language and their posture to communicate a message. On any given day, I can take a look at my dog and know exactly what he needs, and quite often, I know what he is thinking. I can see the love and adoration my dog has for me by his body language. Even without licking and kissing me, he is usually lovingly looking in my direction. He is wagging his tail rapidly to show his approval. He jumps up in my lap, which communicates his playful nature and desire to be close to me.

What's interesting is that most people tend to think that when a dog wags its tail, it is to show how excited he or she is. That is partly true, but it means that the dog is emotionally stimulated which could be either positively or negatively. We have to look at other signals or behaviors to know if our dog is showing stress or showing that he wants to play. One thing is for sure; our pets are communicating with us all the time through their body language. The more we pay attention and learn what stimulates our dogs, the more we understand and can help prevent problems before they even occur.

Humans also reveal so much of their emotions through body language as well. It's estimated that 60% to 70% of all communication happens non-verbally. Learning to read another's body language is a valuable tool to fully understand what a person is communicating. Eye contact, voice inflection, physical posturing, and hand gestures all give major clues about a person's true feelings and emotions. A downward, turned lip can show sadness. Crossed arms can be indicative of how we close ourselves off for emotional protection. Tears show deeper emotions of love, grief, and even joy.

When I engage with another person, I love to look them straight in the eye and give them my undivided attention. I make it a point not to be distracted by others. Nothing is more frustrating than having a conversation with someone while they scroll through their phone on social media, looking for the next person to engage with rather than engaging with the person right in front of them. Eye contact is one of the most important communication tools we have to show others we care about them and value what they have to say. It shows great honor and respect.

I can't help but wonder what kind of body language Jesus used to communicate with others. When Jesus healed others, the Bible says that He was filled with compassion. I often ponder what that looked like as it unfolded. I imagine the person He was healing was able to see so much love and kindness in His eyes. I picture Jesus' hands outstretched to another with a gentle touch. Sometimes words are not needed when you speak from your heart. That is what Jesus did all the time and that is the way I desire to communicate as well. Do you ever think about your body language and what it may be communicating? I've heard it said, "People may forget what you say, but they will never forget the way you make them feel." Your body language is telling your story the loudest. I know I don't always get it right, but I also know I am always trying.

Jesus invites us to take up His mantle and continue where He left off. We should use our body language to extend a hand up or a handout. We can communicate kindness with the deeds that we do. Love is a universal language understood by all that we need to learn to speak. We can begin by speaking it with a smile.

What is the posture of your body? What is the posture of your heart? What message are you speaking to the world by the way you walk, talk, or by your facial expression? Make sure you speak the message you want to portray, and others will never forget you. It's been said, "Preach the gospel at all times; and if you have to, use words."

Therefore, I urge you, brothers and sisters, in view of God's mercy, to offer your bodies as a living sacrifice, holy and pleasing to God—this is your true and proper worship. Do not conform to the pattern of this world but be transformed by the renewing of your mind. Then you will be able to test and approve what God's will is—His good, pleasing and perfect will.

ROMANS 12:1-2

Dear Heavenly Father, thank You for giving me the perfect example in Jesus Christ to show me ways I can communicate effectively. I will earnestly try to follow His example knowing that I am always delivering a message whether I am speaking or not. In Jesus' name I pray, amen.

Time to Paws...

Today I will be mindful of my non-verbal communication style so that I can represent myself and Jesus to the best of my ability as I convey a message of compassion and kindness.

_____

_____

_____

_____

_____

_____

_____

_____

_____

_____

_____

_____

_____

_____

The Unconditional Love of the Father

When I come home from work each evening, my precious dog is there to greet me. He then runs to get his favorite toy and brings it to me. Sometimes he likes to play a game of tug-of-war with me. I know it is because he wants a little more of my time, my attention, and my affection.

No matter what kind of day I have had: good, bad, or indifferent, his love for me never changes. His attitude toward me is not dependent upon my thoughts, my actions, my mood, or my interaction with him. His love and his affection remain steadfast. It is there from the moment I wake up until the moment I go to bed. It is present even while I sleep. Although I cannot see it, I know my dog's unconditional love for me remains throughout the night. It never changes and it never stops. Oh, that I could learn to love like that!

Now, I am sure you know where I am going with all of this, but let's look again at those words I just wrote about my dog. This time, I want you to think about your Heavenly Father's love for you and multiply it by a zillion as you reread these words—no matter what kind of day I have had: good, bad, or indifferent, God's love for me never changes. His attitude toward me is not dependent upon my thoughts, my actions, my mood, or my interaction with Him. His love and His affection remain steadfast. It is there from the moment I wake up until the moment I go to bed. It is present even while I sleep. Although I cannot see it, I know my Heavenly Father's unconditional love for me remains throughout the night. It never changes and it never stops. Oh, that I could learn to love like that!

Friend, God's love for you is constant and steady. It does not fluctuate by your behavior or choices. The love the Lord has for you is never ending and unchanging. It is unconditional because you are His child.

Unconditional love is such a hard thing to grasp. Our very nature as people is that we feel like we must earn anything given to us. We often think that we should perform to some high standard or that we have to look a certain way, or make a certain amount of money, or drive a certain type of car before anyone would see any value in us.

The Bible says that it is man who looks on the outward things. God's love is not like that at all. To say that we are loved "just because" is difficult for many of us to wrap our minds around. I love my dog because he is mine. I love him just because. I could also talk about the love of our earthly fathers, and some of us would have an understanding to a limited degree. Not everyone grew up in a loving and stable environment; and besides that, parents are supposed to love their children.

EUREKA! Now we are talking! God is our Father and our Creator. He is supposed to love His children and guess what? He does. He loves you so much that He counts the number of hairs on your head. He loves you so much that He sings over you and delights in you. He loves you so much because you are His prized possession, His masterpiece.

If I could accomplish one thing in all these messages, it would be that you would know how loved you are. Friend, you are loved. That love is not based on your merit, your pedigree, your actions, your possessions, or anything other than the fact that you belong to God. Whether you acknowledge or accept that truth does not alter the fact that it is indeed truth and you are indeed His. You are so deeply, completely, and uniquely loved. It is a love unlike the love the world can give or even your beloved pet. It is an unconditional love that only a perfect Father can give to you. Unconditional means without condition. (There, I just helped a lot of you when I said it is without condition.) You cannot earn it, nor do you have to. You are loved because you are loved. Our beloved dogs love us unconditionally. They can forgive us when we accidentally harm them, and they also have an extraordinary ability to forget those offenses.

I wish I were so quick to forgive; and equally important, I wish I were able to forget. Did you know that the Bible says that God forgives you and then remembers your mistakes no more?

I have blotted out your transgressions like a cloud,
and your sins like a mist. Return to Me, for I have
redeemed you.

ISAIAH 44:22 ESV

I find such comfort in knowing that I am forgiven and that I have a Heavenly Father who is truly for me. I hope you are comforted with that too. It is because of His undying love and affection for you that He has made a way for you.

. . . .

Dear Heavenly Father, thank You for loving me so much. I am so grateful to know that Your love is not based on my performance or merit; but that You love me unconditionally, not because of what I can do for you, but simply because I am Your child and You are my Father. I receive Your love and forgiveness, and I choose to extend it to others. In Jesus' name I pray, amen.

Time to Paws...

Today I will be mindful that I am loved wholly and completely. I will be reminded of God's unconditional love for me every time I feel or see my dog's unconditional love and affection for me.

_____

_____

_____

_____

_____

_____

_____

_____

_____

_____

_____

_____

_____

_____

Like a Heart

I love to study because I love to learn. I love to learn because I love to teach. I love to teach because it helps people grow and rise higher. I say all of that to tell you that as an avid learner with an insatiable appetite to keep growing and learning, one thing I enjoy is etymology, the study of words and their meaning. I first became interested in this when my then college-aged son would talk with me about the origin and meaning of names. I learned very early on that all names have meanings and were very important and weighty in Biblical days.

When I began writing this book, my friend Natasha encouraged me to look up the original Hebrew name for "dog," and I was delighted with what I found. The word for dog in Hebrew is *kelev*. It is a composite of two Hebrew words: k' meaning "like," and *lev* meaning "heart." So *kelev* means "like a heart." How perfect! I love that the word dog means like a heart. Back in the Garden of Eden, God gave Adam the role of caretaker over the garden and all the animals there. Today we are blessed and entrusted with the role of caretakers for our animals. God then gave Adam the assignment to name all the animals.

> *Now the LORD God had formed out of the ground all*
> *the wild animals and all the birds in the sky.*
> *He brought them to the man to see what he would*
> *name them; and whatever the man called each living*
> *creature, that was its name.*
>
> GENESIS 2:19

I would say that Adam surely got it right when he looked at a dog and said, "kelev"–like a heart. I wonder how long Adam spent studying the animals and their characteristics and nature before he named each one. Our beloved dogs are so loving and carry the heart of a champion, a warrior, and a best friend all at the same time. They truly are all heart! When you have been around as long as I have and you have walked with the Lord for a while, you realize that nothing is a coincidence. All things are very well thought out.

God is the One who spoke order out of chaos and created all things out of nothing. He is the One who overcame the darkness with light. He spoke planets into being, separated the night from the day, and even told the ocean to stay within its borders. The Bible says God created man in His image, and He created the animals as well.

I am so grateful to God for creating me and I am also so grateful that He created you. I am thankful that He thought of everything and created our pets—especially our canine companions. He knew before the beginning of time that our dogs would be full of love. He knew they would help us understand His unconditional love as much as our feeble minds could understand it. God knew that we would have a strong bond with our four-legged family members. The Bible says that God created all things for His pleasure.

The righteous care for the needs of their animals....

PROVERBS 12:10a

Because I love to teach and learn, I know that we can learn a lot from our animals. For example, a cat teaches us about modesty. The ant teaches us about work ethic, and the penguin teaches us about devotion. Undoubtedly, we can all learn to live from the heart like our furry friends.

For me, that is one characteristic that I want to emulate from my dog. I want to be known and remembered for my heart. When others think of me, I want them to remember that I had a big heart that loved and cared about them, the heart of a champion, just like my dog. The state of your heart is so important to God.

In fact, He said in His Word that even though man looks on the outside, God looks directly at the heart. It also says that when we speak, the issues of our heart flow out through our words.

The good person out of the good treasure of the heart produces good, and the evil person out of evil treasure produces evil; for it is out of the abundance of the heart that the mouth speaks.

LUKE 6:45 ESV

What is the condition of your heart today? If it is bruised or broken, the Lord wants to heal it; just ask Him. He is close to those who have broken hearts, and He wants to fill you with His joy once again. If your heart is hardened by the difficulties of life, He wants to remove the heart of stone and replace it with a heart of tenderness. God is always working on our hearts so that we can be known for a heart of love and kindness just like our canine friends!

. . . .

Dear Heavenly Father, indeed, You thought of everything. Thank You for creating the animals so that we could love them and learn about an aspect of Your love. Thank You for letting the name "dog" truly exemplify who they are and what they possess—a heart that is full of love and loyalty. Have Your way in my heart, and please help me to keep my heart open and full of love for everyone. In Jesus' name I pray, amen.

Time to Paws...

Today I will focus on my heart and be intentional to lead with love. I will think about how loved I am and resolve to love others better.

_____

_____

_____

_____

_____

_____

_____

_____

_____

_____

_____

_____

_____

_____

You Belong

When Scout was four years old, we got him a little brother whom my son affectionately named Arrow. At the time, my son was in Boy Scouts and received his Arrow of Light Badge. Before coming to make his home with us, Arrow was in an abusive place where older dogs attacked him, and he was being mistreated. I did not know this at the time, but it made sense when I began to see certain behaviors rise in him frequently in our home.

Arrow was the smaller and younger of the two dogs in our family, but he was much more aggressive. He would often go after Scout and bully him for no reason. Yes, he was playful too, but these acts of aggression came out of nowhere and for no apparent reason. I began to pray for him as I do all my family members. I also asked the Holy Spirit for wisdom as to how best to move forward and handle this situation. One day as I was praying, in my mind, I heard the word "belong." It was so unexpected, but that is what I heard. It popped into my mind out of nowhere, but I knew it was the answer to my prayers. I truly felt it was a word to help my dog. I know that may sound silly to many of you as it did to me as well, but I went with it nonetheless.

I began to talk to Arrow and tell him how happy I was that he was part of our family. I told him that we chose him because we love him so much. I went on to tell him that he did not have to jockey for position or attention because he belongs to this family. I told Arrow that he was loved and valued, and we were so grateful that he came to live with us. It may seem odd to have such a deep conversation with a dog, but what if he could understand, at least in part?

I think we have all felt like we don't belong at some point in our lives. Even now, so many people tend to slip into feelings of loneliness and isolation. We have to fight off thoughts of discouragement and be aware of the questions we ask ourselves: "Where do I belong and how do I fit in?" I know I have asked myself that question numerous times in my life. A sense of belonging, and a yearning for love and security is what every single person needs and desires.

See what great love the Father has lavished on us,
that we should be called children of God! And that is
what we are!

1 JOHN 3:1

Friend, I can tell you most assuredly that you are loved, and you carry great value. Let me remind you, or perhaps tell you for the first time, that you do indeed belong! The Lord loves you with an everlasting love, and the best part is that His love is not based on merit. You are valuable because He says you are valuable. He is the One who says you belong and you will inherit His Kingdom and all His riches. Just like Arrow, when he came to live with us, he became part of our family forever. He became the chosen recipient of everything we could give to him. He doesn't have to earn our love or earn provision; we just give it to him because he belongs to us. He willingly receives all our love, our affection, and our rewards because he is now part of us.

A sense of belonging is something that all people crave and need. It doesn't matter our age, gender, race, or socioeconomic status; we all have an acute need to know that we belong and that we matter. We can belong to a sorority, a church, or a social club; but belonging to someone is so much greater than belonging to something. Hold this truth that you belong to God!

Just like Arrow had to be assured that he belonged, God wants you to know that you belong to Him. You are loved equally and uniquely, because there is no one else like you in all the world.

Everyone on earth is God's creation and we are all loved by Him. When we believe in Jesus and receive His love, that is when we become part of the Family of God. We become heirs to everything He has because we belong to Him.

I will be a Father to you, and you will be My sons and daughters, says the Lord Almighty.

2 CORINTHIANS 6:18

We do not have to jockey for position, or compete with others, or put someone else down to make ourselves feel better. On the contrary, we shine the brightest when we are lifting others up! We are all welcome to go boldly and confidently before God's throne of grace. Just like Arrow didn't have to do anything to receive our love and blessings, we don't have to do anything to receive God's love and benefits either. Always remember, the Lord our God has chosen you and loves you with an everlasting and unconditional love. It is a package deal with great sign-on bonuses and blessings galore that never run out or expire! You are loved, you are blessed, and you belong!

. . . .

Dear Heavenly Father, thank You, Lord, that I belong to You. Thank You for accepting me just the way I am. Thank You for the great inheritance I receive as a Child of the Most High King. Help me to understand fully what that means, and help me to live like a Child of Royalty. Thank You, Father, for loving me and wanting me in Your family. In Jesus' name I pray, amen.

Time to Paws...

Today I will focus on the fact that I do belong and that I am loved! I don't belong to things; I belong to God.

The Importance of Rest

When I was a young girl, I recall hearing the words, "the dog days of summer." I never paid much attention to what it meant back then, but in recent summers I have noticed that my dog spends a little more time sleeping. I can even hear him snoring while my husband and I watch television, and I have recorded him on my cell phone "sawing logs" on numerous occasions. I know he plays hard, and I noticed how he rests hard too.

Just as humans need to get the proper amount of rest, our pets need to rest properly as well. To me, nothing feels better than getting in between two cool sheets after a hard day's work to rest my weary body and mind. Well, maybe a shower after enjoying a day at the beach feels better, but you get my point.

I remember one time when my dog had to be sedated before he had minor surgery. He came home and slept for the rest of the day, as I expected. However, the hard part was keeping him quiet and down the following days so that he could recover. My vet told me the importance of Arrow resting quietly so he could heal properly. The actual term he used was "recovery rest." He said that Arrow needs recovery rest so that his body can have time to heal and mend itself. That term recovery rest resonated with me and has stuck with me all these years.

I believe we all need "recovery rest" from time to time. Life comes at us pretty hard, and sometimes we just need to pull back and take some time out. We need to recover from the week's events. My precious 90-year young father goes to work each day. He gets up about 4:30 a.m. each morning, showers, puts on his suit, drives himself to work, and by 6:30 a.m. he is sitting behind his desk.

On Friday afternoons, he tells me how tired he is and how much the week has taken out of him. He knows the vital role that the weekend plays for him and that is to recover, recuperate, and get the much-needed rest his body is yearning for. What is it about rest, and why is it so imperative that we all get it? I guess I could go back to "In the beginning..." After God created the heavens, the earth, the firmament thereof (whatever that means), and every living creature, the Bible says that God rested.

Now I am no scholar, but if my dog knows the value of rest and my Creator God also set the example to rest, I'd better pay attention. It says that God looked at everything He had done the previous six days and then took an entire day to rest. He didn't just close His eyes for ten minutes—this was serious resting. I find it so fascinating that the One who never sleeps, nor slumbers took an entire day to rest. This tells me that rest is not only about sleeping. I know so often I equate rest to sleeping. However, I realize that I can find rest in reading a good book, watching a movie with my husband, or sitting in church listening to my beloved pastor. True rest is not only found in ceasing from labor, but by being in a position or posture of rest. I heard it explained this way, "We rest in God so we can get the rest of Him." Yes, we need physical rest, but we also need spiritual rest. We need to lay our burdens down at the feet of Jesus and just rest in Him. To me, that is true "recovery rest."

So then, there remains a Sabbath rest for the people of God, for whoever has entered God's rest has also rested from His works as God did from His. Let us therefore strive to enter that rest...

HEBREWS 4:9-11 ESV

Notice that at the end of that verse it says that we should "strive to enter that rest." Wait—what?! We have to work to get to a place of rest?! Well, first of all, you can't rest if you don't first have labor, and second of all, I think we need to receive all the work that God did on our behalf so that we can truly experience the rest He has for us. In other words, we must be intentional on resting. God worked so hard for six days, and then He rested.

We all know that we are at our best when we rest. We can accomplish more and be more productive when we are rested. I am so thankful that the Lord created rest, and He thought it was okay to rest Himself. I wonder how many of us still need to give ourselves permission to rest. Not my dog! My dog knows the value of rest and can rest anywhere at any time. He plays hard and he rests well. I know that I need a 15-minute rest sometime just to unwind and hit reset. (Did you notice the word rest is found in the word reset?) Are you able to settle into the rest of God? I sure hope you are!

. . . .

Dear Heavenly Father, thank You for the blessing of rest and for setting the example that it is okay to rest. Thank You for our pets who don't mind resting at a moment's notice. I will enter Your rest so that I can receive the rest of You. In Jesus' name I pray, amen.

Time to Paws...

Today I receive the rest in the finished work of Jesus. I will be intentional to rest and give myself permission and freedom to rest.

_____

_____

_____

_____

_____

_____

_____

_____

_____

_____

_____

_____

_____

_____

_____

_____

All of You

Scout and Arrow are permitted to enjoy some parts of our home, but there are some areas that are off limits. We do not allow them in our dining room, so we keep it closed off with a wooden doggie gate. We keep the doors to the bedrooms closed to limit access while we are away. We give them access to certain areas of the house but not to all of them. It is safer for them and for us. We feel more at ease knowing the dogs are in our family room and can't get into anything that would not be safe for them. We are comfortable and at peace allowing them to be in that room all the time.

As I thought about this one day, I started wondering. Do we limit and control the Lord's access to our hearts the way we limit and control our dog's access to our home? Ouch! The thought of it made me pause. Sure, we want Jesus to save us and so we invite Him into our hearts and grant Him entrance to the "family room." However, because we have certain issues in our lives that are messy and complicated, we deny Him entry to other rooms. Maybe there's a room in your heart with brokenness from a relationship that went bad.

The hurt is deep so you lock the door and throw away the key.

Maybe you are holding unforgiveness from a betrayal or violation so you've built a fortress around the betrayal, the regrets, the pain and sadness and attempt to lock them away forever. Or maybe there are just some areas of your life that you don't want disrupted like a relationship that you know is not the best one for you, but it's comfortable so it will "do for now." Or you may even be participating in things that you know are not pleasing to a Holy God, but you just don't want to give them up quite yet so you completely shut Him out of that area instead. Been there, done that!

I think we have all been there a time or two, but today I want to encourage you with the truth that I know will set you free. The Lord already knows everything that is hidden behind those closed doors. He knows what is behind "Door #1," "Door #2" and "Door #3." None of those things surprise or startle Him one bit. They haven't discounted your worth or disqualified you. Jesus has not changed His mind concerning you. He loves you with an unconditional and everlasting love, and He wants to bring you to a place of healing and wholeness.

The truth is, none of your pain is hidden from God. The reason He wants access to every single door of your life is so that He can help you clean out the clutter and set you free! You don't need to hoard and hide regret and shame. Jesus wants to make all things new in your life. He is inviting you to open that door and let Him step in and stand in the gap for you. He wants to sit in each room with you as He heals you and comforts you. He specializes in healing broken hearts.

He is called the Prince of Peace, and He can restore those broken parts of your heart right this moment.

Do not be afraid; you will not be put to shame.
Do not fear disgrace; you will not be humiliated.
You will forget the shame of your youth...

ISAIAH 54:4

When I'm not working, my office door is closed because that particular room is off limits to my fur babies. However, when I am in my office working, I allow them in. They just sit at my feet while I work. They don't want anything other than to be with me. I find such peace and comfort having them with me. I believe this is how the Lord sees us. He loves it when we come to sit at His feet. Because He loves us so much, He wants to be with us everywhere we are.

By granting Jesus full access to our lives, we are empowered through our surrender to Him. Our lack of ability to deal with situations gives Him the chance to step in and lift the weight of discouragement and disappointment. By surrendering to Him, all you have to lose is shame, guilt, hurt, fear, deceit, betrayal, and embarrassment. What you have to gain is peace, love, joy, freedom, cleanliness, comfort, and wholeness. That sounds like a great exchange to me! I want that for myself and I want it for you. Moreover, Jesus wants that for you and is inviting you to open up those doors right this very minute. Won't you let Him come in? Let Him in to do a total makeover.

Regardless of your situation, know that He is a good Father, and His thoughts toward you are for good and not evil. He wants to give you a great future and great hope. His love is eternal. His words are comforting. His freedom is for everyone.

* *

Dear Heavenly Father, search me and know my heart. I choose to open up and grant You full access to every single door of my life. Help me be all that You created me to be. I trust You more right now than I ever have and ask that You please come sit with me in each room of my life. I receive all of Your love and peace that will give me great hope and healing. Thank You, Father, for not holding anything against me because I am Your child and You love me with a perfect love. Access granted, God! Come into every single room in my heart and have Your way. In Jesus' name I pray, amen.

Time to Paws...

Today I commit to giving Jesus full access to my entire life. I will not lock Him out of certain areas anymore, but I will give Him full access. I will give Jesus my problems and concerns right away so we can work them out together.

_____

_____

_____

_____

_____

_____

_____

_____

_____

_____

_____

_____

_____

I Have Called You by Name

When Rob was given the joy and privilege of choosing our dogs' names, we wanted him to carefully consider the names that each one would have their entire lives. We made suggestions with his first puppy by asking him to not be in a hurry to name them, but to examine the nature and characteristic of his new family member. For an excited and anxious nine year-old, that took all of ten minutes. I am sure the fact that Rob was a Boy Scout, and scouts are good leaders, helped him name that precious ball of black fur that He lovingly called "Scout."

Scout did exemplify many of the characteristics that a good boy scout exhibits. He was loyal and kind. With a little training and guidance, Scout became very obedient. He was also cheerful and happy all of the time. Like all good boy scouts, our Scout was extremely brave. Yes, our son named his dog very well.

Names are full of meaning. The name Scout is American in origin and means "first and explorer." The name Scout is most appropriate for a dog who always likes to be the leader of the pack or the investigator of the group. One time I even looked up my name, and the name Roxanne means "dawn; bright and radiant star." I love knowing that and I pray that God's light always shines through me.

I remember when my brother Mark took Dale Carnegie's course "How to Win Friends and Influence People." He came home one evening and told me what he had learned. He said to me, "Roxanne, your name is the most beautiful sound you will ever hear." I never forgot that and have made it a good point to remember people's names when I meet them and use their name several times while conversing with them. Inevitably I do remember their names the next time I run into them, and they are always so amazed. Now, I have great news for you today, friend. The Bible says that God calls you by name!

Do not fear, for I have redeemed you; I have summoned you by name; you are Mine.

ISAIAH 43:1b

To be summoned means that you are chosen. Imagine that with me for a moment if you will. The King of all kings has summoned you, He has called you by name and claimed you as His own. Friend, that is not only a big deal, but that is also a HUGE deal! You are chosen and called by name by the Creator of the Universe.

My best friend since kindergarten is named Tricia. One day I wrote her name on the palm of my hand and showed it to her. A big smile came across her face as she opened up her hand. To my utter delight, my name was also written on the palm of her hand. I was astounded and so amazed! Neither of us had talked about it; we just did it. That's what best friends do.

God said in His Word that He has written our names on the palm of His hand as well. I love to remember the story of my friend Tricia and then think about the God of all creation, also engraving my name on His hand. Once it is engraved, it will never wash away. God loves you so much that He calls you by name. You are His precious child, His very best friend. He has written your name on His palm so that He will always have you before Him. My pastor always says, "God has you in the palm of His hand." We have scripture to back that up!

See, I have engraved you on the palms of My hands...

ISAIAH 49:16a

Because you are so precious and valuable to the Lord, your name holds great wealth and meaning to Him. I can imagine the conversations that take place in Heaven about you: "Look at my child [insert name] always showing love and sharing the hope of Jesus with others." Or maybe one of the angels in Heaven is talking about you saying, "Father, look at your child [insert name] praying with that new friend." Not only does God count each star and call them by name, He calls you by name. He chose you as His very own before the foundations of this world were laid. He summoned you and called you by name. You are His!

. . . .

Dear Heavenly Father, thank You for loving me so much and for not only knowing my name, but also calling me and choosing me. When I think about that, I stand so amazed and astounded! I always want to be close enough to You, God, to hear You say my name. In Jesus' name I pray, amen.

Time to Paws...

Today I will be mindful that my name carries weight and value in Heaven because I am so loved by my Heavenly Father. When I hear others say my name, I will remember that God knows my name!

_____

_____

_____

_____

_____

_____

_____

_____

_____

_____

_____

_____

Going to the Groomer

About every two weeks, we take our dogs to the groomer to get a bath; and then once a month they get their hair cut, teeth brushed, a mani-pedi, massage (not really), and come home with a fashionable bandana around their neck that coincides with a near holiday or season. They look good, feel good, and they are exhausted after their big day of getting all spruced up! Shih Tzu dogs are known for their very fast-growing hair which is often kept long. I tried keeping up with their beautiful coats myself at first, brushing them every day as their hair grew longer, but when that turned into a full-time job, I gave it up. I found that if they weren't brushed several times a day, they easily became matted, so I decided to cut their hair short, leaving their ears long and giving their faces an adorable "teddy bear" cut.

They didn't seem to mind, and it sure freed up a lot of time for me! In general, dogs are clean animals. I often see my pooch grooming himself, and I'm glad that he likes to keep himself clean. It reminds me of the saying, "Cleanliness is next to Godliness."

I will never forget one morning I let Arrow out into the backyard to play for a little while. When I called him to come inside, he was covered from snoot to toot in something. When he came closer, I could smell it—feral cat poop! Yuck! I kid you not; it was everywhere. He must have just rolled and frolicked in it. While he was grinning ear to ear, I promise you it was the worst thing I have ever had the displeasure of smelling! I got him shampooed and cleaned up as best as I possibly could, but it barely helped. I knew I needed to call on the professionals.

I phoned our groomer, who usually books up well in advance, and told him of our unfortunate predicament and begged for mercy and an emergency appointment. I was so thankful that he obliged my desperate plea.

My friend, our groomer Lance, promised to clean Arrow up for me and have him smelling as good as new. Without the help of a specialist in that area, there's no telling what would have happened. I was so thankful Lance came to my rescue. I am especially grateful that when we make a mess of ourselves, God promises to clean us up.

Even more than that, when we get so far out in the world frolicking in the temporary pleasures that end up making us smell wretched, God will still cleanse us. Sometimes we look up and realize we are in a pit way deeper than we ever thought possible. We can't ever clean our stains off, but Jesus can. Best of all, we never need an appointment. He is always ready to receive us with open arms when we call upon His Name.

Come now, let us settle the matter, says the LORD.
Though your sins are like scarlet, they shall be as
white as snow; though they are red as crimson,
they shall be like wool.

ISAIAH 1:18

If we will just go to the Father when He calls, just like my dog comes to me when I call, then Jesus will take care of the rest. My dog knew that I would not leave him in that stinky state because I love him too much to leave him dirty! I wouldn't dare snuggle and hold him in that condition, and I didn't want anything to keep him away from me. God feels the same way about you and me. The Bible says that sin separates us from God. He is holy and our sin is a wretched stench to Him. He loves us so much; and He doesn't want anything to keep us from Him, so He made a way to cleanse us and make us new.

The "grooming" or cleansing of the Lord is an ongoing process that begins the moment we give our lives to Jesus. When we receive Jesus as our Lord and Savior, His blood immediately cleanses all our sins, mistakes, failures and disappointments. God chooses to forget those things ever happened! He makes you new. He bathes you in His love and washes you with the water of His Word, but He knows we aren't going to be perfect after that. There are times we will make mistakes or "wander" off and make a mess of ourselves again. The first thing we have to do to get our lives cleaned up is to admit that we need help in doing so.

That is why God sent His Son Jesus to die for us. His sacrifice on the cross is what gives us access to a Holy God. He doesn't expect us to come to Him perfect and beautiful. He just wants us to come and let Him do all the cleaning and grooming. It is amazing how the Lord thought of everything for us.

If we confess our sins, He is faithful and just to forgive us our sins and to cleanse us from all unrighteousness.

1 JOHN 1:9 NKJV

Friend, do you see how much the Lord our God loves you and cares about you? As much as I love my dogs, I know for a fact that Jesus loves you a million times more! He does not want you dirty from your mistakes. He won't leave you out in the "backyard" to try to clean yourself up. Jesus is the best cleaning agent! His blood is more than able to erase all your sins and cleanse you from all unrighteousness. You can come right out of that pit of despair as the blood of Jesus removes even the darkest and foulest of stains.

I learned a song when I was a little girl, and you may know it too. It says, "What can wash away my sin? Nothing but the blood of Jesus. What can make me whole again? Nothing but the blood of Jesus."

If there is one thing you get from this book, know that these words ring true today. If you need to be washed by the perfect and redemptive blood of Jesus, today is the day to be cleansed! Call on Him, ask Him, and believe and receive newness of life today. Don't make the same mistake that I made in my life early on and try to clean yourself up. We cannot be good enough on our own. Be smarter than I was and surrender all to Him right away. Allow the cleansing blood of Jesus Christ to give you a brand-new start and set you on that path to total freedom and victory!

Dear Heavenly Father, thank You for the blood of Jesus that washes away all my sins and mistakes and makes me whiter than snow. I receive Your cleansing power by faith today. Help me to stay close to You. Help me to stay away from the things that pull me off course. Give me a new revelation of Your love and power as I apply the blood of Jesus to my life. Thank You so much for Your grace and mercy that makes me new. In Jesus' name I pray, amen.

Time to Paws...

Today I will choose to stay far away from the temporary pleasures of the world that leave me feeling dirty. I will be mindful that I am made whiter than snow in the eyes of God because of what Jesus did for me.

_____

_____

_____

_____

_____

_____

_____

_____

_____

_____

_____

_____

18

Bright Eyes

As part of my regular care routine, I often check my dog's eyes and ears. When Arrow's left eye began to show signs of an infection, swelling, redness, and discharge, I knew I had to address it immediately with a specialist. I took him to the vet and the prognosis wasn't good. The veterinarian prescribed eye drops to prolong the inevitable. I administered those drops daily and prayed over my sweet Arrow faithfully. I wish I could tell you a miracle happened the way I wanted it to, but that's not what happened. Over time, I saw the cloudiness begin to dim the light in his left eye. We made it a few more years before his left eye became increasingly cloudy, and he lost most of his vision in that eye. I was so sad over this. In fact, I think it bothered me much more than it did him. Even as I write this, I can feel the sadness in my heart and even feel the expression on my face become sad and uncomfortable.

Eyes have always been something that I notice first whether in an animal or a human. The bright blue of my husband's eyes attracted me to him, and I could see light and kindness in them. I love to see the light in another's eyes. It tells me so much about a person without even knowing them. The Bible has a lot to say about a person's eyes too:

The eye is the lamp of the body. If your eyes are healthy, your whole body will be full of light.

MATTHEW 6:22

I think if you break that scripture down, you can tell that eyes reveal a lot about a person before that person even speaks a word. Our eyes let others know what kind of person we are. I can be in a store and see light in others' eyes. Sometimes I will even be so bold to ask, "You love Jesus, don't you?" I get it right 100% of the time, because I can see the light and love of the Lord in their eyes!

Now, what's interesting about Arrow, is that even though he lost his vision in that one eye, the brightness of his soul still shone through. Since Arrow had healthy eyes for so long, he was able to perceive things the way he remembered them. Although his left eye was bad, he never missed a beat and was able to navigate life exactly as he had before.

I love that so much because the way we perceive things affects everything about us. Our perception is our reality. It isn't always what we see; it's what we perceive that matters most. What a powerful principle to take hold of. When we look for the good in people and look for the good in any situation, it affects the way we live. When we see life from the right perspective—a godly perspective, it radiates outward from deep within us. We see with our hearts instead of our eyes which is precisely what I think our dogs do. While a miracle didn't happen the way I wanted, a miracle still happened. Arrow didn't miss a beat in life even when his vision in the natural failed him.

How much more can you and I overcome in this life if we live from our hearts, even when life fails us, even when people fail us, or even when our bodies fail us? How much would our lives change if we always viewed things through the lens of our hearts?

Think about that for a moment. When we look at things through our physical eyes, our brain is hard at work giving us signals and clues to process the information. The sensory receptors in our brain receive and interpret the information, which is what enables us to recognize meaningful objects, events, and people. However, when we look at life through the eyes of our souls, we see things differently. We see people the way God sees them. That right there is powerful and can change our lives if we will allow it.

There is a sweet lady in the Sunday school class that I help lead at my church. She had her sight for most of her life but lost vision in both of her eyes due to a horrible eye infection. Every single week she walks into church with her seeing-eye dog. Although she has never physically seen the classroom, she can perceive the set up in the classroom with the chairs and the podium. Because she was sighted for most of her life, she can truly "see" things as we explain them to her. She has never seen me in the natural, but she tells me often how beautiful I am. I know she is seeing me with the eyes of her heart. She looks so far above and beyond the physical realm and sees much more deeply than the average person. My friend sees people the way God sees them.

I pray that the eyes of your heart may be enlightened in order that you may know the hope to which He has called you ...

EPHESIANS 1:18a

Like my friend, I pray that the eyes of our hearts would be enlightened. Let's not be blind to the beauty in those around us; those who God calls precious in His sight. Allow your eyes to see deeply—way beyond the outer shell. Don't let the brokenness of this world cloud your vision. Live from your heart just like Arrow, because your heart is the real you. Let the brightness from within shine through as the brightness in your eyes.

. . . .

Dear Heavenly Father, thank You for opening the eyes of my heart and enlightening me to see others the way You see them. Thank You for causing me to overcome the world and live from my heart no matter what is happening around me. I pray that I always look for the good in others and help them see the good that You placed inside of them. Thank You for calling me out of darkness and into Your glorious light! In Jesus' name I pray, amen.

Time to Paws...

Today I will be mindful to look for the good in others and point it out. I will be intentional to see people way beyond the physical and look at them with the eyes of my heart.

_____

_____

_____

_____

_____

_____

_____

_____

_____

_____

_____

_____

_____

_____

_____

Come With Gifts

I love coming home at the end of a long day. I know that as soon as I walk through the back door, I will be joyously greeted by my four-legged, tail-waggin' family member. As soon as he hears my car pull up, he runs to his toy basket to grab a toy to present to me. I love presents, and I never grow weary of this endearing expression of his love for me. He has been doing it for years, every doggone day!

Every time this happens, I am reminded of the importance of giving as an expression of our love. Anytime I go to dinner at a friend's house or to a party, I want to take something to show my gratitude. It doesn't have to be an extravagant gift, just a token of love and appreciation. My friend taught me this trait as well. When I tell her I am invited to another friend's house for dinner, she always asks me what I am going to bring as a gift. Last Christmas, I hosted a dinner party at my home for several of my girlfriends, and she asked me what party favor I was going to give everyone. I thought people were supposed to give the hostess a gift! Ha! The point is, while there is such joy in receiving gifts, there is a much greater joy in giving gifts. My dog has this figured out. He's been giving me gifts every single day and sometimes multiple times a day for many years now. I never grow tired of receiving his love offering, and he never grows tired of bringing it to me.

I often think about what gifts we can give that are not really tangible gifts but are beautifully wrapped none-theless. They are the gifts of your friendship, your time, an encouraging word, and your listening ear. Do you know that you have gifts inside of you? When God created you, He created you with purpose and destiny. Believe it or not, you didn't just show up on planet earth by happenstance. The Bible says that before you were formed in your mother's womb, God knew you! The psalmist David says you have been fearfully and wonderfully made. He gave you gifts and talents so you can help and benefit others. Likewise, others' gifts and talents will be used to benefit you.

Each of you should use whatever gift you have
received to serve others, as faithful stewards of God's
grace in its various forms.

1 PETER 4:10

My friend Shawna has many gifts, but her gift of hospitality is above any that I have ever seen. She is an extraordinary party planner and does everything with an over-the-top-amazing flare. Shawna is so much fun to be around and she makes everybody feel so special. She uses the gifts that God has given her to benefit all of those who are blessed enough to be a recipient. Oh, that we would all use what we have been given to benefit those around us!

While it is a great blessing to present gifts to the people we love in the natural, how much more should we focus on presenting gifts to Father God when we come into His presence? Did you know that giving is an act of worship?

We see in Matthew 2 when the wise men first encountered Jesus, "They fell on their face to worship Him, then opening their treasure bags, they presented Him with gifts..." What are the gifts we can give to Him today?

It was Swiss theologian and Catholic priest, Hans Urs von Balthasar, who said, "What you are is God's gift to you. What you become is your gift to God." What gift is fit for the King of kings and the Lord of lords? YOU ARE! Your heart, your mind, your will, and your dedication to Him is the greatest gift He could ever receive! Friend, you are a gift that keeps on giving.

I love that God thinks of me as a present to Himself and then He also decided to deposit gifts inside of me to bless other people. I hope and pray that I discover each gift and talent and use them to the fullest. I hope and pray the same for you too! Remember, giving is an expression of the heart, and you are an expression of God's heart. Let that truth wash over you today and realize that you are a gift to God and a blessing to others with great gifts and talents to share with the world. God designed you that way.

Dear Heavenly Father, thank you for creating me and for placing within me gifts that I can use to help others. Please help me use each of those gifts to the fullest so that I can bless and encourage those around me. Help me to recognize all the gifts that You have given me so I can develop them all! In Jesus' name I pray, amen.

Time to Paws...

Today I will be mindful of the gifts that I have been given and use them to bless those with whom I come in contact! I will not withhold my gifts.

_____

_____

_____

_____

_____

_____

_____

_____

_____

_____

_____

_____

_____

_____

_____

_____

More is Caught Than Taught

When Arrow first came to our home, we were so excited for this new addition to our family. Scout was so happy to have a brother to play with and keep him company. Because Arrow was the younger of the two canine companions, I naturally expected him to learn from his older sibling. But what took place over the years truly surprised me as I watched the two bond and form their little pack.

It started when Scout would come to the back door and greet me with a gift by offering one of his favorite toy stuffed animals whenever I would arrive home. As soon as Scout would hear me turning the door handle to come in, he would run to the toy basket, grab a toy, and dash over to greet me. This sweet and loving gesture brought so much joy to my heart, and I would immediately bend down and give him love and attention. "That's a good boy, Scout! Good boy! I love you too! Thank you so much!" I would say in a slightly higher-than-usual voice as I scratched his back and rubbed his fur all over. Arrow witnessed this exchange between Scout and me and wanted to be a part of it. So one day as Scout was running up to meet me to give me his toy, Arrow came out of nowhere and grabbed the toy right out of his mouth! Then he brought it to me proud as could be and ready for his "atta boy." Arrow was determined to get his accolades one way or another. Of course, he had an entire basket full of toys from which to choose. Who knows why, but he wanted the one toy Scout had. He later learned to come with his own gift, and they both got love and attention.

That wasn't the only way Arrow learned from Scout. Before long, he was copying Scout all the time. When Scout would jump up in my lap to sit and cuddle with me in my recliner, Arrow would immediately get down from the sofa and come jump in my lap to sit and cuddle too. When Scout would keep watch out the front window and bark incessantly to ward off any neighbors who happened to be walking down the street, Arrow would run over and stand next to him and bark all the louder. It never failed, this happened time and time again.

From the outside, this might seem like a game of copy-cat, but it certainly wasn't. Arrow was learning by observing and following the actions of his older brother; and at the same time, he was teaching our entire family how important our actions are.

More than dogs, people are so impressionable, especially young people. Just like Arrow, they are looking for someone to emulate. Often that person is a family member or parent who becomes the mentor. I heard a friend of mine say, "More is caught than taught." I know this to be true in my own life, in our dogs' lives, and especially in the lives of our children.

Children may be tiny in stature, but they are very curious, and therefore, big in perception and observation. What you do speaks louder than any words you could ever say. Actions are powerful, and we must be mindful of them.

They say imitation is the highest form of flattery. I love the fact that Arrow thought so highly of Scout that he wanted to be like him. I am also so very thankful that Scout was such a good boy and didn't have any bad habits to pass down to his little brother. I know other dogs who "caught" bad behaviors just as easily. Just as my dogs demonstrated, the power of influence is tremendous. This also shows us how vital our circle of friends really is. Your circle of friends has a great impact on you, just as you have on them. I read that we are the average of the top five people we surround ourselves with. Think about that for a moment. You are yielding a lot of power, your power, to others. The way we see our success, treat others, and also our self-esteem is directly impacted by those "Fab Five." We must choose wisely if we are going to become all that God created us to be.

Think about your friends right now. Not only should you have mentors in your circle, you should also be a mentor. If you are the smartest one in your group, you need to broaden it. Always remember that your friends can lead you astray, or they can lead you upward.

My beloved friend, Victoria Osteen, is beautiful in every sense of the word. I must say that her outward beauty is a strong reflection of her inward beauty and glow. Victoria is gorgeous. She is strong, yet so gentle. Victoria is wise, never boastful or proud. She is also one of the funniest people I know, which makes her so much fun to be around! She is kind and thoughtful, always looking for someone she can help and bless. As great as her attributes are, the best thing about my precious and beautiful friend is that she loves Jesus with all her heart.

I have observed her closely over the years endeavoring to "follow her as she follows Jesus," and I have become a much better person because of it. I am a more devoted wife and a better mother. I watched how Victoria served her family and I began to do the same. By observing her and emulating her nature, I became a more loyal friend, a more loving and less judgmental Christian.

Victoria never said to me, "Roxanne, do as I do." Instead, she just continued to lead me to Christ by her shining example. Indeed, more is caught than taught! How can I ever pay my beloved friend back for all that she has done for me? The truth is, I can't. What I can do, however, is pass on what I have learned and help someone else become an imitator of Christ.

I want to encourage you to be mindful of the influence you have. Don't lead with a do-as-I-say-and-not-as-I-do mentality. Let's lead our children, and those within our circle of influence, in the ways of righteousness. Let's lead in faith and set an example of love, joy, and forgiveness. As you go about your day, think about what the apostle Paul told his followers:

Follow my example, as I follow the example of Christ.
1 CORINTHIANS 11:1

Dear Heavenly Father, thank You for showing me how to live a life with purpose and meaning. I want to make a difference in the lives of my family and friends and have a lasting effect on future generations. Help me to be an imitator of Christ Jesus and then lead others to do the same. Please show me how to always follow the example of Jesus. Thank You for godly mentors and friends who show me how to live a more excellent way. In Jesus' name I pray, amen.

Time to Paws...

Today I will find someone who I can help mentor. I will live a life of excellence for the Lord and be an example for others to imitate.

_____

_____

_____

_____

_____

_____

_____

_____

_____

_____

_____

_____

21

Fullness of Joy

Have you ever been around someone that you love so much that just being in their presence brings you so much joy? I know I have, and there is not a greater feeling of exuberant joy than being close to someone so near and dear to your heart. Our pets feel the same way toward us. There is always so much joy for our pets and us when we interact! My life has been so enriched by being a pet owner. The time I get to spend with my dog brings me great joy and happiness. His presence is a present to me, and mine is to him as well.

Arrow loves to play, and he is very obvious with his feelings and emotions when we play together. One way I can tell that he is so happy is with his body language. His eyes express joy, and his tail wags vigorously. He enjoys being with me and makes it known. I know there is no place he would rather be than right next to me! As much as our pets express their joy and enthusiasm being in our presence, there is One whose presence is so much greater and brings lasting and eternal joy. The psalmist wrote that in the presence of God is the fullness of joy.

You will show me the path of life; In Your presence
is fullness of joy; At Your right hand are pleasures
forevermore.

PSALM 16:11 NKJV

I wondered what the scripture meant when it said the
"fullness" of joy so I decided to look it up. Fullness means
"the state of being filled to capacity." In other words, in
God's presence we are filled with joy. That means there is
no room for anymore!

So often, we get joy and happiness confused, or some
people use them synonymously; but they are very different. Happiness is great! I love to laugh and be happy. Going
on a trip makes me happy. Being with friends makes me
happy. I've heard it put this way; happiness comes from
what happens around you. Joy is completely different; it's
not based on circumstances. Joy is something so much more
rewarding and fulfilling. Joy is a spiritual force that bubbles
up from the inside of us. Joy is an unshakable sense of peace
that we can have no matter what the circumstances may be.
We can have the complete fullness of joy even when other
emotions are trying to compete inside of us. Joy overcomes.
It is lasting, deep, and abiding. Joy is an eternal gift from
God.

Have you ever noticed how everything your dog does,
he does with great gusto? He eats every single day, but
every time that food goes down, he acts as if it is his first
time to eat! He goes for a walk every day, but the exuber-

ant emotions he displays when it's time to go on that daily walk are far-reaching. When it's time to go in the car, he acts like it's Christmas morning every single time! Our dogs are not shy or ashamed to share their excitement and joy. They always live life from the fullness of joy inside.

I have to admit, I don't.

Too often, humans go through the same motions each day without the enthusiasm we once had. Do you remember how excited you were your first day on the job...or the first day you got your new car...or even the first week you were married? I can bet that after time, the excitement of those new things wore off. However, every day is an exciting new day if we choose to see it that way. Our dogs choose to find excitement even in the most mundane things. It can be the same for us if we take the time to look and see the joy in life each day.

When I was a little girl, my mom taught me an acrostic for the word "joy." She said to me, "Roxanne, to have true joy; you need to put Jesus first, Others second, Yourself last." I never forgot that lesson and have tried to live my life according to this principle—so simple, yet so profound. Joy begins by putting Jesus first.

The Bible teaches us that joy is a fruit of the Holy Spirit's work in our lives. It grows as we walk closely with the Lord, when we put Him first in all of our thoughts, decisions, actions, and words. This is a huge practice and discipline, but it can be obtained, and the results are so worth it!

When we have the fullness of joy, it supersedes all the other competing voices and emotions. Joy is strength.

It gives us sustaining power even in the most difficult times. Joy brings satisfaction, knowing that no matter the circumstances, God is still in control and we can trust Him. Here's another thought about joy: just as our pets are so thrilled to be in our presence, we can experience that same elation when we make it a habit to get into the presence of God! Often, we have to press past opposing emotions or time stealers, but when we do, it isn't long before we begin to just crave being in the presence of God. Then without warning, this deep, abiding, and lasting joy will just exude from every fiber of our being—that's living in the fullness of joy!

- -

Dear Heavenly Father, thank You for the newfound joy that comes from getting closer to You. I want to experience the fullness of joy as I learn more about Jesus. When my pet is happy to be in my presence, I will remember how joyful it is to be in Your presence, and I will make more time to spend with You. I love You so much and thank You for inviting me into a closer relationship with You. In Jesus' name I pray, amen.

Time to Paws...

Today I will be mindful of the acrostic of JOY and apply it to my everyday life. I will spend more time in the presence of God so I can have deep and abiding joy in my life.

_____

_____

_____

_____

_____

_____

_____

_____

_____

_____

_____

_____

_____

Dance in His Presence

In the early mornings before I'm ready to get up, Arrow is often ready to go outside and happy to let me know it one way or another. I get up and take my sweet dog outside for a few minutes and frequently find myself making my way back to my bed. However, some mornings, when I have a little extra time to lounge, I will grab my Bible and notepad and head to the den. Somehow Arrow knows which mornings I'm ready to head to the den, and he begins to jump up and down and turn in circles! It's as if he is dancing in my presence and so excited to start a new day with me. He shows his delight and his exuberant joy by spinning around! My little Arrow has not a care in the world as he twirls and spins. I always love watching his display of excitement and happiness. Not only does it bring a big smile to my face, but it stirs something inside of me to know that I helped bring about this great exhibition of exultation.

I remember when I was much younger and would practice dancing by myself in preparation for the next school dance. Arrow never practices; he just dances and gives it his all. The Bible says that David danced before the Lord, and he gave his all too. I often try to take the time to imagine what in the world that looked like. David was a shepherd boy who became the greatest king in all of Israel. He was so happy that he was able to fulfill something that was in his heart, to bring back the Ark of the Covenant, and when it finally happened, he began to dance wholeheartedly. I am sure there were gasps and eye rolls. How undignified for a man of his stature to dance like a little child without a care in the world.

David was dancing before the Lord
with all his might

2 SAMUEL 6:14b

My dog dances without giving it a second thought every single morning! He raises on his hind legs and jumps up and down. He stands up and twirls in circles like a ballerina. He is so filled with life and joy that he is expressing the overflow of his heart! Oh, to be that free! To dance like no one is watching!

What if we could dance like David, or turn in circles of joy like my dog? Dancing in the Bible was often used as a way to worship and express praise to God. Inside, I want to worship like that. My heart is so full of gratitude and thanksgiving that I want to express it somehow, but how could I let my guard down and act as happy as I feel? "I am a grown woman," or so I tell myself and make an excuse to act dignified. One morning, I let my guard down and danced with my dog. He began to dance even more! As he was filled with more and more joy, it made me all the more silly! I laughed so hard at myself and him, and we both had a great time dancing and twirling! The jubilation was overwhelming, and I began to feel so alive and so free. Sometimes we need to just let loose and release the inner child in us. We just need to dance like no one is watching!

When I was a little girl, we had a black poodle named Piper as our family pet. Piper was not allowed on the living room carpet and he would often step up right to the edge, and even lean over a little, trying to get as close to the living room as he possibly could. My dad recalls a few times when he actually tipped over from leaning so far across the line.

Often when Piper would return from the groomer, he always felt extra special. He would come inside the house and walk straight into the living room without a care in the world like he owned the place! He would then begin to run, and bounce, and leap with pure joy and delight. It was as if he was dancing all around that room feeling clean, special, free, and overjoyed! My dad would always chuckle and then escort him out.

When was the last time you just let loose and danced without inhibition? Like our pets demonstrate and remind us, we should take the time to dance. It is a fun form of exercise which, in and of itself, is beneficial, but it also helps reduce stress. We can meet new people and make new friends by dancing. My sister Annie first met her husband Mike when he asked her to dance, and they have now been dancing together for 30 years.

If our furry friends can dance freely in our presence, we can surely dance freely before the Lord to worship and honor Him. Life is a celebration, sometimes we just need to dance! I double-dog dare you to do it!

. . . .

Dear Heavenly Father, thank You for the gift of dance and the gift of life. It is fun to let our guard down and dance like no one is watching. I want to dance in Your presence as a form of worship overflowing from my heart of thankfulness for all You have done for me. In Jesus' name I pray, amen.

Time to Paws...

Today I will take the time to dance before the Lord as an expression of my grateful heart toward Him.

_____

_____

_____

_____

_____

_____

_____

_____

_____

_____

_____

_____

_____

_____

_____

_____

_____

23

Take Time to Play

No matter the time of day or night, my dog loves to play. He is always ready to play and comes to invite me to join him. Arrow has no regard for the fact that I may be running late for an appointment, meeting, or anything else that I may have on my plate. He does not even care to consider that I have a time constraint; he just wants to play. When I am getting dressed, he thinks it's time to play tug of war with my pant leg. Every single time, he has the same reaction to me putting on my slacks.

If I am making my bed, he will skootch underneath the bed to the other side and beat me over there! Then he scurries underneath again and repeats the cycle playing peek-a-boo. If I ask him, "Where's your toy?" he runs down the hallway into the den and pulls one of his stuffed animals out of his toy basket. Yes, my dog loves to play! I especially love it when he crouches low and lunges at me and then backs off. Then he crouches and lunges again! That is one of our favorite games to play together. I get such a kick out of watching him be so playful and animated. His endurance is much greater than mine, and I tire before he is finished playing, but even still, I take great delight in playing with him and watching him play.

I think we can all learn a great lesson by taking time to play. Our lives are meant to be enjoyed. Even with all the responsibilities that we carry and circumstances that weigh us down, we should still find time to play and laugh. Arrow is a great reminder to me that it is important to incorporate play every day.

I have tried to live this out in my own life. I am an educator, and although I do not teach in the school systems any longer, I love teaching others what I know. I am so thankful for any opportunity to "release the teacher in me." When I became a mom, I wanted to foster a love of learning in my son that I hoped and prayed I fostered in the thousands of students I taught. To do this, I knew I needed to make learning fun for him. I was always dreaming up new ways to incorporate play in our lessons and activities. I remember how I used a deck of cards and taught my son how to play blackjack to teach him mental math skills and statistics. I would have him roll several sets of dice and then have him add them all up quickly in his head. As a young second grade boy, he was becoming quite the card shark! I do believe it served him well, though, because he has always had a strong math mind and is still great with numbers. I will never forget when a friend of mine called me on the phone years ago and said she wanted her son to go to my "math camp" that summer. She hoped that I could teach her son to love math and help him understand higher-level thinking concepts.

I began to laugh and had to come clean with her. She is a pastor's wife, and I didn't think she would appreciate me teaching her young son how to play blackjack or have him roll dice to learn math concepts.

Just as our pets and children make it a priority to find time to play, we need to remember to take the time and incorporate play into our everyday lives, too. Even scripture tells us in the book of Ecclesiastes that we should find pleasure and enjoyment in our hard work. It goes on to say that it is God's gift to us to do so!

That each of them may eat and drink and find
satisfaction in all their toil—this is the gift of God.

ECCLESIASTES 3:13

The city streets will be filled with boys and girls
playing there.

ZECHARIAH 8:5

Not only is playtime beneficial and necessary for a dog's well-being, but it is beneficial to us. Play keeps us active, mentally sharp and alert, physically fit, and happy. When we take the time to play or make learning new tasks fun, we are more apt to retain the information. Taking the time to play not only stimulates our creativity, but it can help us solve problems and adapt better. Laughter and play are good for your soul. Stay young and energetic by taking the time to play! When was the last time you went to a park to watch the children play or even just sat outside to listen to how many different sounds you could hear and distinguish in nature? Our Creator designed so much beauty for our pleasure and enjoyment. He wants us to laugh and feel alive. He said that it is good medicine for our souls to enjoy the pleasures He has given us. Always remember, laughter is good for your heart, so take the time to laugh, and play, and to enjoy your life!

. . . .

Dear Heavenly Father, thank You for the reminder that it is important and beneficial to take time to play. Please help me to remember this and to also give myself permission to laugh and play. Not only will I spend more time playing with my fur baby, but I will also carve out time for myself to play and enjoy life the way You designed for me to enjoy it. In Jesus' name I pray, amen.

Time to Paws...

Today I will carve out time to deliberately engage in fun, laughter, and play. I will make this part of my weekly routine from now on.

_____

_____

_____

_____

_____

_____

_____

_____

_____

_____

_____

_____

_____

_____

_____

_____

Stop and Smell the Roses

I love taking my dog for a casual walk. Have you ever wondered why dogs seem to enjoy that time so much too? It doesn't matter if they are in a state of deep sleep or playing with their favorite toy. Once they hear it is time for a walk, they are 100% engaged, excited, expectant, and ready to go! After I put Arrow's harness on him and we head down the sidewalk, the adventure begins.

Now, of course, I think I am just taking him on a walk for some fresh air and exercise, but he seems to have his own agenda. It is a long and leisurely stroll that he desires to take, lingering over different sights and smells. He doesn't want to miss a single thing and appears to be fully present and fully aware of all his surroundings. He is eager to meet and make friends with the other dogs in the neighborhood. He loves to sniff every single light post, person, or animal that he encounters. He meanders in the beautifully mani-cured lawns sometimes just rolling around in freshly mowed grass. He enjoys this time and takes full advantage of it!

I have learned so much observing my dog's behavior

during our little strolls. By watching him, I learn what it's like to linger and to be fully present in the moment. Arrow takes the much needed time to stop and give his full attention to each smell, every detail, and each person. He does not allow one person to pass him by without making sure they know that he has made an effort to try to engage with them.

Oh, how we need to learn this life lesson! Every single day, we pass countless faces as we set about to fulfill and complete our assignments and agenda, but do we stop to take time to "smell the roses" so to speak? I wonder what would happen if we were more intent on leaving a lasting impression on those with whom we come in contact as opposed to allowing them to casually pass us by. What are we missing out on by letting others pass us by without any interaction whatsoever? More importantly, who are we missing?

When we take time to be fully engaged and fully present, we position ourselves to receive the blessings and beauty God has given us. Arrow showed this to me, and now I am intentional on taking the time to pay closer attention to all my surroundings and the people in it.

I endeavor to go through my day and gather a "bouquet of roses" which are my acknowledged blessings each day. Of course, I have Jesus as the center of my bouquet, and He is the One I start the day's new arrangement with every day. I am so blessed to add the roses of my husband and son. As I add a new rose to the colorful and beautiful display, I take the time to recognize the gift and blessing that each one represents. It becomes an act of worship as I acknowledge and express my deep, abiding gratitude for the blessings of family and friends as well as a myriad of other things that become a part of my daily bouquet. The fact that I am healthy and can take my dog for a walk is a great flower to add. I don't want to exclude the job that I have been given, the home I have to live in, or the church where I worship. I heard someone say before, "What if the only thing you have today is what you gave thanks for yesterday?" That is a great reminder to not take people or opportunities for granted. Don't allow the everyday favors and blessings to lose their sparkle in your eyes. Being grateful for the people God has placed in your life, and speaking that gratitude out loud, is powerful and keeps our thoughts refreshed.

Now, we have to remember that every rose bush that produces beautiful blossoms also has thorns all around. We have to be careful not to focus only on the thorns. Yes, they hurt. Yes, they surprise us sometimes. Yes, life can be tremendously difficult during the pruning season. However, if we would all take the time to focus on the blooms coming forth and their fragrant offerings, we could manage everything much better. God has given us so much to enjoy, and it is up to us to take the time to recognize and be grateful for those things instead of taking those blessings for granted or casually passing them by as insignificant.

Every good and perfect gift is from above, coming down from the Father of the heavenly lights, who does not change like shifting shadows.

JAMES 1:17

Just as Arrow has reminded me to slow down and enjoy the beauty of people and the blessings of the Lord in my life, I hope you are reminded to do the same. The job that you have is a rose given to you from God. The family you have to love is another rose. The fact that you have a roof over your head and food on your table are all flowers the Lord continually gives to you daily. Adorn your table with this robust and fragrant floral arrangement. Let it be the centerpiece of your heart and give God thanks. Your gratitude and thanksgiving are fragrant offerings that you can give back to Him. Always remember to stop and smell the roses!

Dear Heavenly Father, thank You so very much for all the blessings you give to me daily! I will savor each one like a beautiful bouquet of fresh flowers. I commit to stop and breathe in the moment, enjoy the aroma, and be grateful for everything You have done for me. In Jesus' name I pray, amen.

Time to Paws...

Today I will be mindful of the blessings I have, gathering them like a large bouquet of roses, and placing them on the centerpiece of my heart.

_____

_____

_____

_____

_____

_____

_____

_____

_____

_____

_____

_____

_____

_____

_____

No Place Like Home

I heard that when a person loses their beloved dog, they have a 93% chance of finding him within the first twenty-four hours. After that amount of time, it goes down to a dismal 60% chance. Like most things, timing is of the essence. However, we should never give up hope. I know several stories of dogs getting lost who were later reunited with their owners. These stories are always so heartwarming. I heard a story about a dog who was away from his owner for twelve years when he was spotted in Pittsburgh under a man's shed over 1,100 miles away from his home in Florida. He still had his original collar, so the man contacted the owner who immediately got in her car and drove for days to be reunited with her family member.

I heard another story of a lady who lost her dog after it slipped out of its collar on a walk around Central Park and ran away. The owner plastered the city with "Lost Dog" posters and responded to several sighting reports that ended up being empty leads. She also had a ground crew scouring the land for her precious dog to no avail. One day, she was putting up a sign when a few ladies passed her by and said they would pray and ask Jesus to find her dog for her. A week later, the dog was found!

My sister lost her dog for several months. When all hope seemed lost, out of the blue, Ralphie walked up the driveway completely carefree. Ralphie had no idea of the trauma and sadness that his momma and daddy had been experiencing. Nonetheless, all of that went out the window because there was much jubilation when Ralphie came home.

That is how our Heavenly Father must feel when we come home to Him. I think many of us have lost our way a time or two, at least. It could have been our own doing that got us off course and led us astray. Sometimes we drift ever so subtly that we don't even know we have wandered far away from home, and we are lost. Sometimes it is just flat out rebellion that makes us turn away. Whatever the case may be, God is always looking for us and longing for us to return home.

There's a story in the Bible about a young son who wanted his inheritance so he could go party and have a grand time. He took the money and left his father's home. After the money and the fun ran out, the young son was all alone. He took a job feeding pigs, only eating what the pigs didn't eat. Finally, he had enough of living this way and decided he would go home and ask his dad to please give him a job as a hired hand. He felt certain that he had disgraced and embarrassed his father because of his behavior. The Bible says, however, that as he was getting closer to his house, his father saw him from a long distance. His dad was so elated that he ran out to his son and hugged and kissed him, and even threw him a party. I can picture that dad waiting by the door every single day looking, hoping, and praying that his son was okay and would make his way home.

Just like Ralphie was celebrated when he made his way back home, the son was celebrated when he returned home, too. How much more does God celebrate us when when we make our way back home to Him?

> But the father said to his servants, "Quick! Bring the best robe and put it on him. Put a ring on his finger and sandals on his feet. Bring the fattened calf and kill it. Let's have a feast and celebrate. For this son of mine was dead and is alive again; he was lost and is found." So they began to celebrate.
>
> LUKE 15:22-24

Notice that not once did the dad jump all over his son, scold him, or belittle him. His joy was that his son was home!

I don't know where you are in this season of your life, but can I please remind you that God is waiting for you to return home to Him? He is not mad at you and will never belittle you. He rejoices when one lost sheep is found. How much more will He rejoice over you, His precious son or daughter?

Maybe you are close to your Heavenly Father and that is wonderful! However, could you reach out to one who is far away and needs some encouragement and guidance to get back home?

Every one of us needs to help the lost ones get home. Whether it has been 12 years or 12 hours, there is no place like home for home is where the heart is, and home is where our loving Heavenly Father wants all His children.

. . . .

Dear Heavenly Father, thank You for always welcoming me back home. Thank You for Your great love, mercy, forgiveness, and overwhelming kindness. I will not wander far from You again for that is where I feel most secure and loved. I love You, Lord. In Jesus' name I pray, amen.

Time to Paws...

Today I will make my way back home to God and help others who are lost to find their way back too. I will tell them of Jesus' love and forgiveness for them.

_____

_____

_____

_____

_____

_____

_____

_____

_____

_____

_____

_____

_____

_____

_____

_____

Your Inheritance

I was utterly amazed when I learned that an estimated one million dogs, in the USA alone, have been named as the primary beneficiaries in their owner's wills. I read that one lady in Italy left about $13 million to a stray cat she found. Another multimillionaire in Dallas has arranged to leave over $75 million of his fortune to his beloved dogs. Now that really proves that "things are bigger in Texas!" One can set up what is known as a "Pet Trust" to make sure their faithful four-legged family and friend receives the life insurance premium. Of course, a trustee and a caregiver are still needed to care for the pet, but little Fido will have the standard of living to which he is accustomed. You may be surprised to know that the world's richest dog is a German Shepherd named Gunther IV. His father, Gunther III, was left $65 million. That just goes to show that every dog does indeed have his day! That can sure buy a whole bunch of milk bones!

Did you know that you too have a great inheritance? An inheritance is something that is promised and passed down to a named heir after the person dies. As the children of God, we have been made joint-heirs with Jesus. We receive the same inheritance that Jesus does. The apostle Paul tells us that it is an inheritance that will never spoil or fade.

The Spirit Himself bears witness with our spirit
that we are children of God, and if children,
then heirs—heirs of God and joint heirs with Christ,
if indeed we suffer with Him, that we may also
be glorified together.

ROMANS 8:16-17 ESV

Although an earthly inheritance can wither away, and vast sums of wealth can vanish over time, our inheritance in Jesus Christ will never run out! Our Father owns everything, and you have been named His heir.

And you also were included in Christ when you heard
the message of truth, the gospel of your salvation.
When you believed, you were marked in Him with
a seal, the promised Holy Spirit, who is a deposit
guaranteeing our inheritance until the redemption
of those who are God's possession—to the praise of
His glory.

EPHESIANS 1:13-14

As God's children, we have been adopted as sons and daughters into the Family of God. We are heirs and co-heirs with Christ Jesus. Everything that Jesus receives we receive. This inheritance is irrevocable, meaning no trade backs. What do we receive? We receive forgiveness, eternal life, all the promises of God contained in His Word, and ultimately, a place in Heaven that Jesus has been preparing for us. What do we have to do to receive this inheritance? This incredible inheritance is promised to all who believe in Jesus Christ—God's own Son who came to earth, died on a cross for our sins, and rose again on the third day, overcoming death, hell, and the grave so that we can live forevermore. We inherit the glorious riches by believing in Jesus and receiving Him as our Savior.

My husband and I have one son who will receive everything once we go live in Heaven full time. Our son is not working for this inheritance, he gets to receive it all as our precious child. It is our great joy to bestow upon him whatever we have.

Because I have received Jesus as my Lord and Savior, I know that I am a child of the Most High King. I am royalty with an eternal inheritance that the Bible describes as something that no eye has seen, no ear has heard, nor human mind has even been able to conceive the things that God has prepared for those who love Him. I have no idea all my inheritance entails, but as a daughter of royalty, I am going to walk with a little swagger and be cordial and loving to everyone. I am going to invite them to join me in this great inheritance by putting their faith in Jesus. I am also going to walk a little taller and straighten my crown.

Isn't it amazing to know we have an imperishable, undefiled, and unfading inheritance kept for us by God? The Holy Spirit, who helps us, teaches us, and trains us, is but a deposit of what is to come. Think about that for a doggone minute. The very Spirit of God who lives inside every believer is a deposit guaranteeing our inheritance! That fires me up so much! It makes me want to howl at the moon and bark like a dog! If you are a follower, then you are an heir and co-heir with Christ Jesus. Like me, you can cry, "Abba! Father!" Get ready to receive your inheritance!

. . . .

Dear Heavenly Father, thank You for choosing me to be a joint heir with Christ Jesus as Your child. I know I could never do anything to earn such a great inheritance, so I want to thank You as I simply receive all You have for me. I will do my best to help others come into their inheritance as I share the Good News. In Jesus' name I pray, amen.

Time to Paws...

Today I will be mindful of who I am in Christ Jesus as an heir. I will also help others put their faith and trust in Jesus and become a rightful heir of His.

_____

_____

_____

_____

_____

_____

_____

_____

_____

_____

_____

_____

_____

_____

Wag Your Tail Not Your Tongue

One afternoon I was having a conversation with my dear friend Regan, and she told me something her beloved mother used to say about their family dog. She would say, "The reason a dog has so many friends is because he wags his tail and not his tongue." To me, that is such a funny saying and one I had not heard before our conversation. What a powerful point! An entire book could be written on the importance of holding our tongue, not just one devotional, but let's talk about it for a minute.

In both dogs and humans, the tongue is an essential part of our bodies. It helps us drink and eat. Dogs use their tongues to kiss their owners. (I will leave that alone!) A dog will also use his tongue to lick his wounds because it has antimicrobial properties. The tongue on a dog acts as a built-in air conditioner to cool their bodies down. After you see your dog running and playing, you see his tongue hanging out and he is panting. His tongue often becomes bigger as the blood flow increases. In humans, the tongue is one of the strongest muscles we have. It is controlled by nerves that come straight from the brain. Maybe that is why we should think before we speak.

The Word of God has a lot to say about the tongue because God knows what it can do. The Bible says that the tongue has incredible power. The writer of Proverbs says that both life and death are in the power of the tongue. We can speak life, hope, and encouragement to others by the way we use this very powerful tool. Similarly, we can tear a person to shreds by the words we speak. We can curse people or bless them with our tongues.

As a little girl, when someone said something mean to me or my siblings, we often retaliated by saying, "Sticks and stones may break our bones, but words will never harm us." As an adult, I know that's not true. I mean, how deceitful is that? Words do harm us and frequently leave deep wounds that may never heal without the help of the Holy Spirit.

I think of all the writings about the tongue, James talks the clearest about it:

> *Take ships as an example. Although they are so large and are driven by strong winds, they are steered by a very small rudder wherever the pilot wants to go. Likewise, the tongue is a small part of the body, but it makes great boasts. With the tongue we praise our Lord and Father, and with it we curse human beings, who have been made in God's likeness.*
>
> JAMES 3:4-5, 9

Those verses say so much. Although our tongue is small in size, it is enormous in power. Our tongues can direct others toward the way that leads to righteousness, or it can be used to lead others down the wrong path. A little white lie is a lie, nonetheless. Every lie matters.

The Bible tells us, "Out of the abundance of the heart, the mouth speaks." Gossip, slander, lies, and unwholesome talk are all ways we "wag" our tongues too much, and when we do those things, we get in agreement with the enemy of our souls. I don't want to line up with the enemy. I want to line up with the Giver of Life! I want to speak kind words that refresh people's souls. Kind words build up. Kind words are like a soothing ointment that brings healing. It is like honey to the soul, the scriptures tell us, both to those who speak and those who hear. Kind words are life-giving, loving, and encouraging.

A dog is a friend to man because he can keep his tongue in check. We all could learn a great lesson by doing the same. Let's speak words of life over people. We have enough people talking down to us, speaking words of defeat and death over us, and telling us what we can't become. Let's praise our God and lift His creation, His children, who have been made in His image.

Let's train our tongue to speak pleasant words, and if we can't find anything nice to say, the best thing is to not say anything at all. Take a lesson from dogs—wag your tail and not your tongue!

. . . .

Dear Heavenly Father, I come to You thanking You for reminding me of this truth that I know sets me free. Lord, I give You total control over my tongue now and forever. Please help me to train it in a way that is pleasing to You so I can be a blessing to those around me. Help me to think before I speak and ask myself if this helps or hurts. I know I can't do it without You, and I thank You for always empowering me to do the right thing. In Jesus' name I pray, amen.

Time to Paws...

Today and every day, I will think before I speak. I will only say words that encourage others and bless them. I will use my tongue to speak life to those around me.

_____

_____

_____

_____

_____

_____

_____

_____

_____

_____

_____

_____

_____

_____

_____

Work in Progress

My good friend Larry told me a story about something that happened during a dog obedience class. One of the larger dogs attacked a much smaller dog. The smaller dog was okay, but the owner was naturally upset. In fact, the owner of the smaller dog demanded that the bigger dog be put down. The trainer didn't think that was necessary and pleaded with the smaller dog owner to drop the charges and give him some more time. The trainer agreed that what happened was horrible and expressed his remorse. He then said something to the owner of the smaller dog that changed everything. He said, "He is still in training. I am not done with him yet."

That's how it is with each of us. God is not done with us! He sees the value and the potential that He placed inside of every one of His children. While we see others in process—in the messy stages and all the brokenness and upheaval, God sees us as the finished product, all cleaned up and transformed in the image of His Son, Jesus. He sees us with great possibility and potential, just the way He designed us.

Dogs need training for their safety and for the safety

of those around them just like we do. Well behaved and disciplined dogs experience less stress and interact better with other dogs as well as people outside of their families. Furthermore, a well-trained dog forms a stronger bond with his owner. Training is necessary if we want to communicate with our dogs.

Just like our pets, while we are in training and need more time to develop discipline and structure, we need to be mindful that others are in training as well. They may have a long way to go, or they may have surpassed us. That doesn't matter. What matters most is to realize that we are all in process and on our way to becoming everything God intended for us to become.

Training is not easy, and discipline is not fun. We don't like to be told "no" or stretched beyond our comfort zone, but we do like the result, and that's what we need to focus on as we discipline ourselves.

No discipline seems pleasant at the time, but painful. Later on, however, it produces a harvest of righteous- ness and peace for those who have been trained by it.

HEBREWS 12:11

As a good parent, I disciplined my son. I didn't discipline him because I was mad at him; I corrected him because I love him. I wanted to keep him safe. I wanted him to grow and mature and make his mark on this earth in a favorable way. God is a good Father and disciplines His children because

He loves us. He disciplines us so that we will grow spiritually and develop a more personal and intimate walk with Him. Even though I didn't always get it right with my son, our Heavenly Father gets it right with us every single time! When it comes to disciplining us, He is conditioning us for a fruitful and blessed life.

While we can't always control our circumstances, we can control our attitude and heart response. We have to realize we are continually a work in progress. No matter our age, we must make sure that we stay humble, teachable, and trainable. You really can teach an old dog new tricks, and I am living proof of that! I was 40 years of age before I started living a life that was completely sold out to the teachings of Jesus and following His example. I grew up in a Christian home and regularly went to church. However, it took me a very long time to realize that following Jesus fully was where my true joy and identity were found. I was finally able to see what it meant to have the abundant life found in Christ Jesus. All along the way, I was teachable, but I wasn't putting it into practice. I wanted to grow and learn but didn't live it out day to day. That has changed for me, and I am so grateful to God for His patience with me!

Friend, we need to be patient with others while they are on their way to becoming all that God created them to be. Just like we are patient with our puppies when they're being house trained, or our children when we potty train them, let's be patient with others while they are being trained in character and godly living. Nobody needs to be reminded of what they are doing wrong. Most people know full well when they are off course. What they really need is your encouragement. They need you to love them right where they are. They need to be reminded of their God-given potential. If the God of all creation can love them right where they are, so can we. Let's do our part and then watch and see what the Lord will do!

. . . .

Dear Heavenly Father, thank You for Your great patience with me as I grow and become all that You created me to be. Help me to encourage myself and others to keep growing in wisdom and practice all that we know to do. I want to be a great example to others as I follow the example of Jesus. I am so excited about my future, Lord! I love You and thank You! In Jesus' name I pray, amen.

Time to Paws...

Today I will be an encourager to others and remind them that they can become everything God created them to be. I will be patient with those who are in process and love them in the midst of it all.

_____

_____

_____

_____

_____

_____

_____

_____

_____

_____

_____

_____

_____

Thunderstorms

Every single time a horrible storm comes near our home, our dogs shudder at the very first crack in the sky that explodes with a thunderous roar. As many times as it has occurred, they have still not gotten used to the startling shock and all the noise that accompanies each storm. Immediately, they run to me to find shelter, security, and peace amid such commotion.

Of course, I always do my best to console and comfort them. I use a very gentle voice and stroke their backs softly and rhythmically to help them regain their solace. I remind them how much I love them and that I will protect them.

The loud thunder of a storm reminds me of the enemy of our souls who makes so much noise and racket to try and startle us and get us off course. That ol' liar and deceiver has a bark that is much worse than his bite, and he is not afraid to use it. He is strategic with his attempts to instill fear into us. He sends storms into all our lives, and we must do exactly what my dogs do—run for shelter to the only One who can comfort us and bring us peace.

Friend, Jesus is the Peacemaker in every single storm that rages in our lives.

I have told you these things, so that in Me you may
have peace. In this world you will have trouble.
But take heart! I have overcome the world.

JOHN 16:33

Look at this verse carefully. Right before the part that says, "In this world you will have trouble" is an incredible revelation and powerful promise. First, we see that we can have peace in Christ Jesus. In the middle of storms, difficulties, sadness, and upheaval, we can have peace. The Lord Jesus then warned us that we would have trouble; we will go through trials and storms, but we are to take heart and be comforted because He has already overcome all of them. Storms will come, and storms will go. The way we perceive them affects how we are going to walk through them.

My dogs want to be connected and close to me during storms, and they want security and peace. That is what we all want and need during the storms that blow through our own lives. The only way to achieve that is to run to Jesus and let Him shelter us and protect us. Storms aren't there to break us, to scare us, or to have us shrink back in fear. Quite often, the Lord in all His sovereignty, will use those very same storms to make us stronger. Those storms are there to fortify us, strengthen us, and to conform us into the image of Jesus. As difficult and painful as they can be, storms equip us to help ourselves and others.

Just as my dogs run to me for protection, we need to run straight to God every time a storm arises, or the enemy is shouting accusations at us or hurling insults. We can always press into God for help and comfort. Storms have a way of refining and even reigniting our faith. Quite often, storms become the launchpad for great growth. Adversity tends to stretch us and causes us to trust God even more. As much as we all despise the storms of life, they truly play a vital role in our refining process. We can prepare for the worst, but we should expect the best. During the tough times, seek God first and then lean on friends and family to help you. It is in those most trying and difficult times that the very nature of God is revealed, and we become more like Jesus.

Have you ever noticed after a storm how green and peaceful everything looks? Yes, there may be some debris scattered here and there, but for the most part things look vibrant and new. There is a fresh smell in the air. Circumstances around us may be in a whirlwind of commotion, but the realization of God's presence in all of it brings us great peace. Peace is not the absence of storms; it is knowing that God's presence is riding out the storm with us.

Do you know why dogs tend to be scared of thunder? They are mostly afraid of thunder because they do not understand what it is. They hear the loud noise, and it frightens and startles them. Isn't that just like us? We are afraid of the unknowns and the what ifs? The enemy of our souls can make so much noise that it startles us, and we become terrified, even though we are not even sure what it is that is so terrifying! Research shows that 95% of the things we fear don't even occur. To help calm our dogs in a storm, experts say we should turn on the television or some music to help drown out the noise. I would suggest the same thing for humans. When the enemy is thundering lies and accusations in your ear, run to God, who is your strong tower and ever-present help in time of trouble. Turn up some praise music really loud and begin to sing your way through the storm! When you turn your worry into worship, I assure you that the frightening chatter will end. When a storm rages and tosses you to and fro, find a few scriptures that will help anchor you to hope and calm your spirit. The Prince of Peace is always there for you, and He will bring peace in the midst of any storm.

* *

Dear Heavenly Father, thank You for inviting me to run to You during the storms that rage in my life. With You, I don't need to be afraid. I will find peace and comfort as I lean on Jesus, who is with me during every phase of my life, especially the storms. I will turn on praise music, read my Bible, and pray until the storm passes. As I do, I trust that I will get closer to Jesus and become more like Him. Thank You for loving me and helping ease all my worries and cares. In Jesus' name I pray, amen.

Time to Paws...

Today I will remember that storms aren't here to break me, but they will help me become a stronger person. I will remember that Jesus is my Strong Tower and Safe Shelter during any storm that rages.

_____

_____

_____

_____

_____

_____

_____

_____

_____

_____

_____

_____

_____

For Your Protection

Every pet owner has experienced his pet getting into something that they shouldn't have. A while back, my brother-in-law had to rush his dog to the emergency vet. The dog got into one of the children's Easter baskets and gobbled up every chocolate bunny, egg-shaped chocolate, marshmallow bunny, and all the colorful foil that surrounded them! Not only did this make the dog very sick, but it could have caused him to lose his life. I am sure the dog was not thinking a thing about consequences as he over-indulged. He wasn't concerned about the danger of it all or anything of that nature. All he was thinking about was gulping down the forbidden delicacies as quickly as he could!

Isn't it like that with us at times? We see something that we want even though we know it is not good for us, which could include so many things from overspending, drinking too much, or even entering into a relationship that we know is not the best for us. We don't think much about the fallout, the aftermath, or the effects; we just go for it because it feels good at the moment. Maybe we even participate in acts that we know we should not be doing, vowing to ourselves to do better next time. Then the "next time" comes and we give in to the same temptation again.

The Apostle Paul understood this. He knew he had been forgiven so much, and he genuinely wanted to do the right thing, but often he found himself stumbling over and over again. Read what he wrote in the book of Romans:

> *I do not understand what I do. For what I want to do*
> *I do not do, but what I hate I do. For I do not do the*
> *good I want to do, but the evil I do not want to do—*
> *this I keep on doing.*

ROMANS 7:15, 19

To do, or not to do, that is the dilemma. One thing I can say for certain is at least we are in good company! Paul had a radical conversion when he encountered Jesus on the road to Damascus. He went from being an enemy of God to writing over two-thirds of the New Testament. However, he still struggled with what we all struggle with—pleasing our fleshly desires.

Can I tell you some good news today? There is enough grace to forgive all our sins and mistakes. There is also enough power to overcome all life's temptations. We just have to choose to turn away from those desires that are not beneficial to us, and not pleasing to our Heavenly Father. When we resist those things, it kills the desire until, eventually, it is no longer a temptation. Just as we keep poisonous foods and dangerous products away from our pets, our good and loving Heavenly Father wants to do the very same for us. A good parent always wants the best for his child and wants to protect him from any harm.

One night, when I was a teenager, I was headed to a party. I drove through a park where all my high school friends would typically hang out, but I wasn't supposed to go there. In fact, the last thing my parents told me as I left the house that evening was, "Do not go to the park." Well, the first thing I did when I left the house was drive straight to the park. I didn't think it would be a big deal. I wasn't planning to stay long and then I would go to the party.

When I left and pulled out of the parking lot of that park, my car stalled in the middle of the road. I don't remember anything else that happened that night. All I know is that five days later, I woke up in the hospital with tire tread imprint across my face. Witnesses say I got out of the car, and when I did, I was rear ended and run over by my own vehicle. The car knocked me down, fracturing my skull, rolled over my face, and dragged me twenty-four feet down the road. I was trapped underneath the car with the exhaust resting on top of my leg. After two surgeries and three weeks in the hospital, I was back home. I still have a horrible scar on my leg. If I had only heeded my parents' simple warning, I would not have been hurt.

Just as we protect our children and animals from certain things, God gives us boundaries to keep us safe and out of harm's way. Sometimes we can look at those boundaries and get upset, not realizing that they are there for our own good and protection. I don't think the Lord is trying to keep us from having fun, He just knows full well the consequences of some choices we make, and He wants to keep us from such harm and danger. The pleasures of this world are many, and many are very costly because they can make you spiritually sick. If you can have a made-up mind ahead of time about some of the temptations that will come your way, it will be easier to say no and keep on walking by. The temptations will indeed come, but you can overcome them all. God promises to provide a way of escape. Sometimes that way of escape is a simple, "no."

Friend, God is always faithful and will never give you a test that you cannot pass. He made you a winner and an overcomer, and He will always order your steps for your protection!

. . . .

Dear Heavenly Father, thank You for protecting me. I know that when I face temptation, You always provide a way of escape for me. Please help me do the things I know I should do and stay away from the things that I shouldn't do. I do not want to keep repeating the same cycle that produces the same miserable results. Thank You for being such a good and loving Father who wants the very best for me. I love You. In Jesus' name I pray, amen.

Time to Paws...

Today I will be mindful of Your protection. I choose not to repeat destructive patterns. When I feel tempted, I will cry out to God to help me, and then I will plan my escape route.

_____

_____

_____

_____

_____

_____

_____

_____

_____

_____

_____

_____

_____

At Your Service

The multiple blessings and benefits we have as dog owners are simply amazing! Not only are our pets loyal and loving family members, but many of them are specially trained to provide a specific service to their owners. Over 80 million Americans have the companionship of a service dog specifically trained to help with a disability. Dogs provide a plethora of pleasures to us as man's best friend, but service dogs are invaluable, providing the lifeline to their owner's day to day lives.

Guide dogs help their sight-impaired owners navigate their environments. Individuals with hearing difficulties can have a service dog who is specifically trained to alert them of important sounds. Some dogs are trained to remind their owners to take their medication or provide incredible comfort and peace for those suffering with a psychiatric condition. There are even dogs who can smell and detect cancer! People who have disabilities are now able to augment all aspects of their lives thanks to their amazing service dogs. Not only do these canines provide much love and companionship to their owners, but they can also boost self-confidence and morale.

When the City of Houston experienced unbelievable flooding from hurricane Harvey in 2017, tens of thousands of people had to abandon their homes due to the rising flood-waters. Many of the neighboring churches opened as make-shift shelters to give Houstonians a place to stay warm and dry and to be fed until they could get back home. My family and I were volunteering at our church when my son's room-mate brought in his emotional assistance dog. I will admit it was the first time I ever saw a dog in church, so I wasn't sure what to expect. However, his highly-trained dog was so calm and friendly. He was very smart and obedient. He was also able to perform his job well as he comforted children and adults alike who were affected by this stressful situa-tion. This precious service dog was not easily distracted by his wants and whims; he stayed focused on his goal to serve and comfort others.

What an excellent example to us to stay focused on the needs of others too. Being in service to one another is one of our highest callings as believers. When you serve others, you put their needs above your own. You go out of your way to be good to people and help them. Serving others is a basic principle of the Christian faith. Jesus, who is God in the flesh, served people everywhere He went. He always made time for them, healing them, feeding them, and even washing the feet of His disciples. The Bible implores us to serve others. We are to pray for one another. We are to encourage one another. We are to help each other, care for them, and on and on. We are the hands and feet of Jesus on the earth, and when we serve others through our loving acts of kindness, it is a reflection of our relationship with God and our love for Him.

Serving others isn't just a blessing to the other person; there are also tremendous benefits for us. Serving increases the quality of our lives and gives us a deep sense of purpose. Serving others teaches humility as you take the focus off of yourself. Serving brings great joy and satisfaction, and it helps reduce stress. I can now really understand what Jesus meant when He said, "It is more blessed to give than to receive."

Each of you should use whatever gift you have received to serve others, as faithful stewards of God's grace in its various forms.

1 PETER 4:10

One time I found myself in an uncomfortable situation, and I had a big choice to make. I could either serve a person who had been talking poorly about me, or I could just blow them off. I have to be honest with you—I did struggle with my decision, but decided to take the high road and be the bigger person. I helped that person with his needs and went about my business, not giving it another thought. A few days later, I was in church singing at the top of my lungs when I heard a familiar voice inside of me say, "You passed the test." I had no idea where that came from and was so startled. I thought to myself, "What test?" Then I heard a reply, "The greatest in My Kingdom is the servant of all." Immediately I remembered the uncomfortable situation I was in a few days prior, and I knew my choice must have pleased the Lord.

Friend, pass the test—serve others. Just as your dog faithfully brings you a toy or the newspaper and serves you with such joy, be one who serves others faithfully and with great joy. You can never give to others without the Lord taking notice. We all want our lives to matter, and serving others is a direct way to make your life matter! Look for ways to bless and help others, whether they are familiar faces or strangers. Do so with a joyful heart and disposition. Know that God has already equipped you with every good and perfect gift that you need to serve His children. It pleases His heart when you use those gifts to serve and help others.

. . . .

Dear Heavenly Father, thank You for the opportunities I have to serve others. Help me to discover all the gifts that You have given me so that I can use them to help other people. Let me be on alert to see who I can serve and how I can help continually with a joyful heart. In Jesus' name I pray, amen.

Time to Paws...

Today I will find someone I can serve and help. I will do this often and be intentional in my service to others. I will start with my family and branch out to my neighbors and co-workers as well.

_____

_____

_____

_____

_____

_____

_____

_____

_____

_____

_____

_____

Man's Best Friend

I read that it was King Frederick of Prussia who first called his beloved greyhound "man's best friend." In the instant that those words were recorded, they have remained true and constant for generations. Why would one choose an animal to be a best friend? What makes a best friend the best anyway?

One of the very first traits I look for in a best friend is loyalty. I want someone who will be with me through thick and thin, a friend who celebrates with me on the mountain top, and helps me in the valley. I love a friend who will be loyal no matter what because that is the type of friend I am.

Another trait I look for in a friend is someone who has a good listening ear. Sometimes we don't need an answer or reply, we just need someone to listen with their heart while we sort out our feelings and thoughts. It doesn't take a genius to know there is a reason we have two ears and only one mouth. We should do twice as much listening as we do talking. That part I am still working on!

I can't think of anytime in my life that my dog has not

been loyal to me or that he has ever failed to listen to my every word. If I walk from one room to the other, he is right by my side. He is always ecstatic to see me walk in the door. He brings me his best toy, his favorite possession in all the world. His enthusiasm is never half-baked or generated. It is real and authentic. Oh, if we could just remember to treat others with the same affection and love that our dogs treat us with every day!

Whether I am dressed to the nines in my finest attire or lounging in my favorite pajamas and slippers, it makes no difference to my dog. He thinks I am the greatest thing ever. A best friend is just like that as well. Like my best friend, my dog loves me just the same whether I am dressed up or not. When I am sick or just not feeling well, he never leaves my side. If I am happy, he is happy. If I am grouchy, he is still happy! (Although he will express concern.) I could go on and on, and I am sure you could add so much more to this as well. A best friend loves in all times regardless of the season we are in or our frame of mind.

A dear friend will love you no matter what, and
a family sticks together through all kinds of trouble.

PROVERBS 17:17 TPT

However, I want to tell you about a friend who truly is "man's best friend." As a matter of fact, the Bible says that Jesus is a friend that sticks closer than a brother. His love and approval of you are pure and unconditional! Jesus loves us all the same whether we are in our pajamas or dressed to the nines. He loves us unconditionally whether we are on the couch being a grouch or in the street being sweet! His love does not fail or falter regardless if we are living our best life and shining our very brightest or living a pitiful life and loathing in darkness.

A man who has friends must himself be friendly, but there is a friend who sticks closer than a brother.

PROVERBS 18:24 NKJV

I know the Lord is always happy to see you and spend time with you. Of all the riches of the world, time is the one thing that we cannot make more of. We all get the same 24 hours each day. That is why it is so important to start your day with your thoughts focused on God and His plan for your life. If there's anyone I want helping me plan my day and chart my course, it would be my best friend, Jesus! I know His plans are for my good, and His ways are so much higher than mine.

Can I just be real with you for a minute? Sometimes I feel a little guilty about receiving so much love and adoration from Jesus. I know it is because, in the natural, we often feel that love must be earned to be merited. We have a mindset that we have to look a certain way or talk a certain way. We think we have to always be on our "best" behavior. With people, that very well may be the case, but Jesus' love is opposite. Unconditional means just that—His love is without condition. The truth of the matter is that we could never do enough to earn or merit His love. I want to put a new and true thought in your mind and free you right now: our best would never be good enough! I am so happy to report that it doesn't have to be because His best is more than enough, so we are off the hook!

We have a free pass just to believe and receive. I know it sounds too good to be true! It is true, and it still sounds too good and too easy. What did you ever do to earn such unmerited favor and love? The short answer is...nothing. You don't have to earn it! My dog pours his love upon me "rover and rover," and I never question it. Why, then, is it so hard for me to believe that a loving and merciful God would not also want to pour His love upon me?

The next time you walk into your home and your dog comes running over to see you with his tail wagging, I want you to think about Jesus. More than your very own pet who is thrilled to see you because he loves you so much, Jesus is so happy to see you and be with you. It is His good pleasure to give you His love. He lavishes it upon you. Lavish means to give extravagantly and generously. Can you just soak that in for a moment? The Creator of the Universe loves you extravagantly. His love for you is immense, and it is forever.

The love of Jesus never changes because He never changes. He is the same yesterday, today, and forever. All He desires is you, not part of you, but all of you. He wants the good, the bad, and the ugly because that's how much He loves you. You are God's best friend, and He wants to be yours!

Dear Heavenly Father, teach me how to receive Your love without condition. Thank You for Your great love for me and for being patient and kind to me during different phases of life. Thank You for loving me simply because I am Your child. Thank You for being a friend that sticks closer than a brother, and the One who loves me more than my dog loves me. I love You too! In Jesus' name I pray, amen.

Time to Paws...

Today I will think about how much Jesus loves me. When I see the love my dog has for me, I will focus on the greater love that God has for me. I will be mindful to receive love and also reciprocate it.

_____

_____

_____

_____

_____

_____

_____

_____

_____

_____

_____

_____

_____

33

Loyalty

Dogs are pack animals who work together to protect one another. They will even give their lives for another member of the pack. The mere fact that dogs are pack animals makes it evident that they are incredibly loyal. There is also a scientific reason that they are so loyal. Loyalty is crucial for pack animals, which is how they overcome harm and danger by working together. To your loyal dog, you are his family, his pack, and he will always protect you.

I am sure the fact that we feed them and give them a nice place to live helps encourage their loyalty, but it is also true that they see you as a vital member of their pack, and they will go to the ends of the earth for you.

I read a story about one extremely loyal Akita dog named Hachiko (Hachi) who was owned by a Japanese man named Ueno. Every day, the two companions would walk to the train station where Ueno would catch a train to work. Hachi would wait at the station all day for his owner to return. This went on day after day for several years until one sad day, Ueno suffered a brain aneurysm and died while at work. He never made it home but Hachi continued to wait for Ueno for over nine years until he died at the station from natural causes. Today there is a bronze statue of Hachi displayed outside that train station in honor of this incredibly loyal canine.

Always remember, your dog loves you wholeheartedly and would do anything for you. Loyalty is true devotion and the ability to put others before yourself. Let me ask you this: who is in your pack? Who are you loyal to? Who would you go to the ends of the earth for today?

Notice that loyalty isn't about the other person, it's about you. Our dogs are loyal no matter how we act because their loyalty stems from deep within their character. We should be a loyal friend to others and especially our family members. A dog never stops to ponder whether or not you deserve their fierce loyalty and affection. They do not withhold their love from you. They just act. I believe that loyalty is the most important and cherished quality in a relationship. I strive to be a loyal friend, and I look and long for loyalty in return in my relationships. To me, honesty and loyalty go hand in hand. If you are loyal, I know I can trust you.

When things are not measuring up and circumstances are challenging, you need that loyal friend to turn to in those moments. For me, I have found that loyalty in my older sister Shavonn. Shavonn is my safe place to fall when times are hard. Even if she were not my sister, my heart would have searched her out. She is a true and loyal friend. Your heart knows when you find a trustworthy and loyal friend because they make you a priority and not an option. Shavonn always takes the time to listen to me with her heart and has my best interest in mind. A friend who will stay loyal in the good times and bad, like Shavonn, is a treasured gift. On top of that, she inspires me to rise higher, too. That is one of the best things about a loyal friend. They inspire you to become the best version of yourself.

As spectacular as a loyal friend is, the true definition of loyalty comes from God Himself. He alone is the epitome of loyalty because even when we fail, even when our friends fail us, God will never fail us. His is faithful—the same yesterday, today, and forever. He will never be anything other than faithful and loyal!

Just as God is so faithful to us, we should be as faithful and loyal to Him. We should love the Lord our God above everything else and everyone else. One way to develop loyalty to God is by reading His Word. When you get to know Him through the scriptures, you get to know the nature of our wonderful God and loving Father. We are a blessed people because God is loyal to His promises and covenants. His Word is true, and it is life. Jesus shows us the way to God and lives a perfect life that we can and should emulate. Jesus was loyal to His Father. Be loyal and faithful to the calling of God on your life.

Know therefore that the LORD your God is God;
He is the faithful God, keeping His covenant of love to
a thousand generations of those who love Him and
keep His commandments.

DEUTERONOMY 7:9

When I was a teenager, my dad taught me one of the greatest lessons in life. He said to me, "Roxanne, you did not get to choose where or when you would be born. You didn't choose your family or the color of your eyes. However, one thing you do get to choose is what kind of person you will become. Being a person who chooses honesty, loyalty, and integrity is all up to you, and no one can take them from you. When you choose, choose wisely." Those words impacted me deeply, and I have never forgotten them.

There was a time when a man's "yes" and his handshake were as secure as a binding contract. People knew how to be loyal to their word and reputation. Make sure that you are always the kind of person who sticks by your words. When you give someone your word, don't change your mind or trade them for the next best deal. Let your word be your bond. Be loyal to others, God, and yourself. Loyalty is not just a word, it is a lifestyle. Like our beloved pets, and especially like our loving Heavenly Father, be loyal to the end. I promise, you will never regret making this choice.

. . . .

Dear Heavenly Father, thank You for showing me what true loyalty looks like in my life. I want to be like Jesus and keep my word. I want to be a person of noble character—faithful in all things. I especially want to have loyal friends, and I desire to be a loyal friend to my family, friends, and especially You. Thank You for such a great lesson that I will carry with me for the rest of my life. In Jesus' name I pray, amen.

Time to Paws...

From this day forward, I will work to become the most loyal and faithful person I know how to be. I will let my *yes* mean *yes* and my *no* mean *no*. I will be a loyal and trusting friend and family member.

_____

_____

_____

_____

_____

_____

_____

_____

_____

_____

_____

_____

_____

Never Left Out

Every morning when I wake up, I let Arrow out into the backyard. If I leave the back door open, he will go and take care of his business. However, if it happens to be a cold morning and I close the door ever so slightly, he just sits right outside the door and waits for me to open it without him ever going potty. For some reason, he is always so afraid that I am going to leave him out there. I love him and would never deliberately leave him out.

I have thought about that so much. What is it in our nature that has us thinking we will be left out? Why do we worry about being left out or overlooked? I know it must be because we all have an innate need to be included, to be counted. We do not want to be left out or feel as if we have been abandoned. We all experience "FOMO" or fear of missing out, but we don't need to!

From the very beginning of time, God made it a point to include you. Everything He has ever done has been with you on His mind. The Bible says that before God ever formed you in your mother's womb, He knew you. He took great delight in making you His beautiful masterpiece!

> *For You created my inmost being; You knit me together in my mother's womb. I praise You because I am fearfully and wonderfully made; Your works are wonderful, I know that full well.*

PSALM 139:13-14

As I stated in an earlier lesson, dogs are pack animals. It is their natural characteristic to run in packs—they need to be in relationship. They love to be together all the time.

Do you know that we were created for relationship as well? Our Creator God is a very relational and personal God. He knows you so well that He has counted every single hair on your head. Sometimes I look at my hairbrush and wonder how many recounts God had to do that morning after each stroke of my hairbrush.

When God formed the first man, Adam, He looked and said it was not good for Adam to be alone so He made Adam a helpmate. God was in a personal relationship with Adam and Eve from the very beginning. He never left them out. He always counted them in.

We know the story where Adam and Eve sinned against God thereby breaking their unique relationship. God was not satisfied with a broken relationship, so He had another plan. Jesus, the Son of God, is the One who has bridged the relational gap between a Holy God and man. Once again, we can have relationship with God the Father through His Son Jesus.

Just like our dogs will always be relational because of their very nature, we are the same way. We were born to be in relationship with one another, and with Jesus, our Lord.

When my relationship with my husband or a family member is out of sync, it is usually because my relationship with Jesus is out of sync too. The Lord esteems loving relationships and places them in high regard. One way I picture this idea in my mind is to envision a cross. My relationship with God is the vertical axis. My relationship with others is the horizontal axis, and Jesus is the center of it all!

In the same way we develop and build relationships with our pets, our family members, friends, and coworkers, God wants us to be intentional to develop our relationship with Him too. The closer we are to Him, the more we take on His very nature and character. The more we are like Him, the more we can see others through the Father's lens of love and forgiveness. We not only see others with the same value that our Heavenly Father sees them, but we love them the way He loves them.

Before we know it, we can love all people better. We can invite our friends, family members, and even strangers and include them in this amazing community known as the Family of God.

How beautiful is that! No one is left out! Everyone can reach someone. Friend, let me remind you that you are not discounted, disqualified, or overlooked. God has counted you in from the very beginning. He wants to be in relationship with you more than anything. You are never left out!

Dear Heavenly Father, thank You for creating me and for inviting me to be in relationship with You. I want to have a great and loving relationship with You. Please help me have healthy and strong relationships with all my loved ones and especially my relationship with You. In Jesus' name I pray, amen.

Time to Paws...

Today I will remember that I was created to be in relationship with God through His Son Jesus. I will continually work
to cultivate and nurture all my relationships, especially my
relationship with my Heavenly Father.

_____

_____

_____

_____

_____

_____

_____

_____

_____

_____

_____

_____

_____

Not Yet

What is it about waiting that seems so unbearable at times? We have all grown so accustomed to having things right away and pretty much at the tap of a button. In reality, we spend most of our time in life waiting. We wait for that special someone to come into our lives. We wait for the day when we graduate from college. We wait to get married. We wait to start a family. The key is this: be sure and wait well, for in due time, you will reap the benefits.

How can we wait well? We can wait well by preparing ourselves. We can do the "next thing" that gets us one step closer to the desired outcome. We can pray and talk to the Lord about our desires, dreams, and expectations. We should wait patiently and without complaining. We should wait trusting that God knows what is best for us. I especially love to wait with expectation knowing that He is a good Father who knows how to give great gifts at the perfect time. Waiting can be a blessing as we learn to wait well and allow the Lord to do something within us.

But those who wait on the Lord shall renew their strength; They shall mount up with wings like eagles, They shall run and not be weary, They shall walk and not faint.

ISAIAH 40:31 NKJV

Maybe that promotion at work has to come after your supervisor gets a new position. Perhaps the Lord is not bringing your future spouse to you right now because you still have some growing to do, or maybe that person isn't ready for such a prize like you. Trust Him when He says, "Not yet, we still have to wait a bit!" Wait well and prepare yourself while you wait.

Some things are worth the wait. When my son was born, he came an entire week after his due date. I had October 4 as his arrival date in mind for nine long months. My doctor examined me and said, "Not yet, we still have to wait a bit." When October 4 came and went, the next seven days seemed like an eternity—a bloated, uncomfortable, waddling, hot eternity. I knew that God knew what was best, and I wanted that for my son too. However, I was also so anxious and excited to see my son. My son Rob was worth the wait. All of the promises of God are worth the wait.

I am amazed that my dog seems to have a built-in alarm clock. Whether it is time to take him on a walk, feed him dinner, or go to bed, he knows the hour, and he is ready.

One fall day, it seemed Arrow missed the memo that it was Daylight Savings Time, and we had turned our clocks back one hour. He thought I was late taking him for his afternoon walk. He evidently was very well aware of what time it was and stood by the front door looking at his leash, barking periodically as if to say, "Hello! Mom, it's time!" I had to keep saying, "Not yet, we still have to wait a bit." He seemed so impatient.

Sometimes I get that way with God. I get impatient waiting for a breakthrough that isn't happening on my timetable, or while I'm waiting for His promises to manifest in my life. I want them, and I want them right now! Actually, I wanted them yesterday. I can imagine hearing the Father say the same thing to me that I say to my dog, "Not yet, we still have to wait a bit."

Arrow knows when it is 5:30 p.m. whether it is Daylight Savings Time or not. He is ready for his dinner at 5:30 p.m. sharp. He will bark and whine if I am late. I wonder what God thinks about all of my whining when I feel it is time for something. As a parent and a pet owner, we may not respond well to whining, and we may even give in. However, I'm certain whining doesn't change God's timing one bit!

Yet the Lord longs to be gracious to you; therefore He will rise up to show you compassion. For the Lord is a God of justice. Blessed are all who wait for Him!

ISAIAH 30:18

Friend, I know your Heavenly Father has huge blessings in store for you. I know He is as excited to give them to you as you are to receive them. Trust His timing. If you feel the Lord saying to you, "Not yet, we still have to wait a bit!" trust that it is for your own good. God's delay is not His denial. Don't grow weary or sad while you wait. A good Father not only knows how to give good gifts, but also when to give them. The Lord loves you so much and wants to give you great gifts at just the right time. Be blessed as you wait for Him and wait well by preparing yourself.

. . . .

Dear Heavenly Father, today I declare that my trust and hope are in You. Even when things aren't working out on my timetable, I trust that they are working out on Yours. I know You will give me everything I need at just the perfect time. While I wait, please help me grow and mature so that I can receive Your blessings with a grateful heart and be ready for such gifts and treasures. I will wait well and prepare myself for the coming blessing. In Jesus' name I pray, amen.

Time to Paws...

Today I will be mindful that waiting is really a blessing and not a curse. I will slow down and be patient as I prepare myself for the goodness of God to arrive at the perfect time.

_____

_____

_____

_____

_____

_____

_____

_____

_____

_____

_____

_____

_____

_____

36

Hidden Treasures

I love to watch my sister Jennifer's dog receive a treat from his mommy. Her precious Pomeranian named Riley gleefully accepts the treat with eager enthusiasm and delight and then goes straight to the same hiding place and buries his treasure there. It doesn't matter if Jennifer gives him a new toy, a chewy bone, or another treat, it always results in Riley going and burying his newfound treasure in the same spot.

What is it about treasure that we all want? I remember as a young girl going on hunts for buried treasure. My siblings and I would hide a small trinket of some kind and then make a map that would be used to unveil the surprise. Even to this day, there are television shows that follow men and women on expeditions to the four corners of the earth to find buried treasure far beneath the sea. You can even go on a vacation and pay money to pan for gold! It seems as if young and old alike enjoy the hunt and the idea of a prize to be found.

I am sure many of you, like me, enjoy various earthly treasures. These could come in the form of a fancy house, money, a fine car, a prestigious job, possessions, jewelry, or even significant influence. Those things are great blessings for sure, but there are treasures the Bible talks about that have nothing to do with the treasures of this earth.

Do not store up for yourselves treasures on earth, where moths and vermin destroy, and where thieves break in and steal. But store up for yourselves treasures in heaven, where moths and vermin do not destroy, and where thieves do not break in and steal. For where your treasure is, there your heart will be also.

MATTHEW 6:19-21

That last line is the key to this verse and the way that each one of us should live our lives. What we value is directly reflected in how we live. When Jesus is your treasure, you will devote your entire life to living for Him and bringing Him great glory and honor. As a result, your life will produce such great fruit, and you will reap incredible blessings far beyond any earthly treasure.

How could one possibly store up riches in Heaven? When your relationship with the Lord becomes your priority in life, then you will begin the Heavenly treasure hunt. Building an intimate relationship with Jesus through the Word of God is one way to get started. Go after the higher calling on your life. Live a life that is holy and blameless before the Lord. That is a hard discipline, but one that is obtainable. Before you do or say anything, ask yourself, "Does this honor God?"

A quick self-examination can be done in a moment's notice and help establish a new thought life and pattern for yourself. Be good to people and generous with your love, your time, your encouragement, your wealth, and your resources. These are all things that are pleasing to the Lord. Good works do not get you to Heaven; only the blood of Jesus does that. However, good works are a by-product evident in the life of a faithful follower of Jesus.

You've probably heard the saying, "I've never seen a hearse with a U-Haul." It's true. You can't take your earthly treasures with you. You can, however, store vast wealth and treasures in Heaven that will last through all eternity. The bottom line is this: people who follow Jesus should treasure Jesus. Where is your heart, friend? That is where your treasure is stored. Like Riley, let's build a stockpile of treasures and good works that will impact people and last forever.

. . . .

Dear Heavenly Father, thank You for this sweet reminder today to store up treasures in Heaven. I know I can do that by growing my relationship with You and by being so loving and kind to Your creation. Jesus, You are absolutely the greatest treasure of my life, and I am so grateful to You and for You. Help me become all that You created me to be. In Jesus' name I pray, amen.

Time to Paws...

Today I will begin the journey of a lifetime as I am mindful to store treasures in Heaven each day. Holy Spirit, I ask You to help me achieve this and focus on what matters most.

_____

_____

_____

_____

_____

_____

_____

_____

_____

_____

_____

_____

_____

_____

Give Us This Day

I was in my kitchen one morning getting my coffee ready. My dog Arrow was with me and watching me intently. I looked down at him and asked, "Would you like a treat?" He started turning around and around and was so excited! I gave him his little treat which he inhaled with pure joy and delight.

When I give my dog a treat, it serves multiple purposes. It is enjoyable for both of us because I see how happy it makes him. Also, I know the treat is good for him, strengthening his bones and cleaning his teeth. It is a sweet way for me to bond with my canine companion whom I love so very much!

After I gave him a treat and saw that he was wagging his tail rapidly with eager excitement, I chuckled and laughed out loud. What a joy it was for me to bless him with a little nugget. At that moment, I looked over and saw my communion elements that I keep in a dish on my counter. As I looked at the grape juice and cracker, I said to myself, "I think I will have a treat too!"

As I reached for the communion cups, it made me think: What if I was as eager to receive the Lord's cup as my pup is to receive from me? What if I was as excited about that special treat from the Lord as Arrow was about his special treat? The act of communion is a great gift that we get to participate in as we remember the death and resurrection of our Lord Jesus. The Bible says that we are to do it often, and as we do, we are to remember Him.

In an earlier devotion, I wrote about Arrow's left eye becoming increasingly cloudy. My sister Jennifer told me how her little Pomeranian, Riley, had a hair loss disease, and she began to share communion with her dog. Now, this may sound unconventional, but we have to remember, God made a covenant with all His creation. His original intent in the Garden of Eden was to commune with all living creatures. Scripture says, "Let everything that has breath praise the Lord." I believe our pets are created to give glory to God, just like all His creation.

Do you know what happened to my sister's Pomeranian? After a few weeks of praying and sharing communion, all of his hair grew back! I thought that I would do the same thing with Arrow knowing the power that I receive when I take part in communion.

I began to receive communion with Arrow each morning. I always take the time to consider the bread and the juice, which represents the body and blood of our Lord and Savior Jesus. The body of Jesus was beaten severely on His way to the cross. The Bible records that those lashings He endured are what gives us our healing. I believe that is multifold. We are healed physically, emotionally, spiritually, and financially. The prophet Isaiah spoke these words 400 years before Jesus went to the cross:

> *Surely He took up our pain and bore our suffering,*
> *yet we considered Him punished by God, stricken*
> *by Him, and afflicted. But He was pierced for our*
> *transgressions He was crushed for our iniquities;*
> *the punishment that brought us peace was on Him*
> *and by His wounds we are healed.*

ISAIAH 53:4-5

As I prepare the elements and pray and give thanks to the Lord, Arrow watches me so intently. His eyes are fixed on me, and he is looking up at me as I pray and give thanks to the Father. It's almost as if he truly understands. He is so still before the Lord. I break the wafer and put part of it in my mouth and part of it in Arrow's. Then I take the little cup of grape juice and give thanks to the Lord for the cup of salvation, the new covenant that I have entered in with Him. I drink it and then give the last little drops to Arrow. I thank the Lord for His healing of Arrow's eye as I pray.

After the first week of doing this, I noticed that Arrow's eye was not as weepy. I also noticed that the blue discoloration and the cloudiness in his eye began to dissipate and that his normal brown color was returning. His eye is so much better today and I can't wait to share his full healing!

I know some people might think it is a coincidence, but I do not believe that for one second. God has shown His power and all surpassing greatness in my life way too many times for me to think anything is a coincidence. Even to this very day, Arrow and I continue to receive Holy Communion together each morning as I pray over Arrow and our family.

Friend, don't you know that if God will take care of my dog and heal his eye, He will surely take care of you, His precious child? You are His prized possession and master-piece whom He loves with an everlasting love. He is such a good Father who cares for His own. The Bible tells us that He watches over us, so be comforted and strengthened with that truth.

* *

Dear Heavenly Father, thank You for the gift and the privilege of receiving Holy Communion. Thank You for permission to partake of the body and blood of Jesus often and to recall the many wondrous acts that Jesus did for me because You love me so much. I believe the words spoken by the prophet, "By His stripes I am healed!" I drink from the cup of salvation so that I can live forever with You. In Jesus' name I pray, amen.

Time to Paws...

Today I will begin to make it a practice to receive Holy Communion in my home. I will remember what Jesus did for me at Calvary. By His stripes, I am healed. By the blood He shed for me, I am saved. I believe it and receive it!

_____

_____

_____

_____

_____

_____

_____

_____

_____

_____

_____

_____

_____

For the Health of It

I never realized when I set out to get a dog that it would have such a positive effect on my overall health and well-being. I have observed my little four-legged friend engage with me, others, and his doggie friends. In doing so, I've become more aware of the affirming influence these loving little creatures can bring to our homes and lives. Could it be then, that God uses our pets to help bring balance to the imbalanced things in our lives?

Health is a serious concern in today's society. If you don't believe me, just watch television or listen to the radio for a few minutes and you will realize exactly how bombarded you are with health suggestions. You will hear things like:

"Take this in order to achieve that."

"Do this and you will live longer."

"Your life will be so much better with this gadget in it."

There is so much information out there that it can be difficult to keep up with it all. Plus, it rushes toward us through so many sources and with more speed than ever before. Infomercials and television shows introduce us to new products daily. It can be overwhelming.

I want to offer you some hope today that doesn't involve pills, shakes, gadgets or gizmos. The fun fact is this—studies have shown that you can achieve major health benefits just by owning a dog. In addition, many of the benefits of having a furry friend around are achieved immediately! How fun is that?

I was thrilled when I found out that being a pet owner reduces blood pressure, lowers cholesterol and helps lower triglycerides. This is needed to help improve cardiovascular health. So, my observation then is this—it is all good news, because this could only mean one thing. Owning a dog reduces the risk for heart attacks!

Seriously, let's count the benefits of simply taking our beloved dog for a moderate walk 20-30 minutes each day. First, it can provide enough exercise to help us lose weight and keep us more fit, active, and mobile. Next, it allows us an opportunity to interact with other pet owners who are out for their morning stroll. Can someone say improved social life? Yes, please! Although, I don't recommend adapting the greeting methods of your pet (they smell each other). A simple, "Hello, nice to see you ..." will suffice!

As a dog lover, one of the greatest health benefits is that my dog helps reduce my stress levels and helps me feel happier. I love coming home from a hard day and just getting in the presence of my loyal companion. Think about petting your dog, stroking their back, scratching their ears ... it's almost like each stroke brings increased calmness and happiness to us. What about those times when they come and curl up next to you? Oh, I love that! It's like their little bodies are just sucking all of the negativity right out of you and replacing it with love and goodness.

Research shows that simply being near your pets can help you decrease anxiety. Did you know that dopamine, the hormone known as the "pleasure hormone," is triggered when we spend time interacting with our dogs? Not only do we receive immediate satisfaction as dopamine is dispersed, but I also found out that it aids in supporting our long-term memory. I don't know about you, but that's exciting for me! Why? Because it means having a dog can help me remember where I put my keys last night! You don't want to forget that tip!

Another added benefit to pet ownership is that you are less likely to suffer from depression. Seratonin is known as the "happy hormone" and is released when we play with our pet or engage in activities with him. Seratonin is discharged when we are cuddling with our dog, stroking him, or even playing a game of fetch. There are too many good hormones being released into your body for depression to stay! The love and companionship of our dearly-loved dogs aids us in so many ways. Being a pet owner and pet lover makes us too blessed to be stressed and depressed!

The truth in all of this is that we were created for relationship. Our pets bring so much love, joy, and peace to our lives. It is the joy we find in the relationship with our pets that produces the fruit (or benefit) of improved health and overall well-being.

Similarly, there are great benefits to being in relationship with other people. God created us for relationship. First and foremost, God created us to be in relationship with Him through His Son Jesus. When we receive Jesus into our hearts, we are also given the Holy Spirit who teaches and comforts us. Our relationship with the Holy Spirit is to receive Him as a mentor or teacher. I can't think of anyone better than the Spirit of God to teach me. Likewise, Holy Spirit is also known as a comforter, one who is always there for us during difficult or challenging times. How many of us need some real comforting these days especially when times are so tough?

When we are in healthy and loving relationships, we thrive. Being in community and relationship with others will always have challenges. We are humans after all. The benefits, however, far outweigh the difficulties. Our canine family members help us keep the balance in these things. When we pay attention, they can also remind us about loyalty and love. They seem to have cornered the market on all of the right kinds of benefits!

Two are better than one, because they have a good
return for their labor: If either of them falls down,
one can help the other up.

ECCLESIASTES 4:9-10a

We need our friends and family members around us to help share our burdens. It can help reduce the weight of the load on our own shoulders and cuts the burden in half. When we have the support of those around us, it provides reassurance that we are not walking through life alone, we have security in God and His care for us. Plus, we have the support of those around us.

Similarly, when we are able to share our blessings and milestones with others, it seems to multiply the rejoicing and makes the celebration so much more satisfying! Double the joy! Double the fun!

There was a scientific study that showed the human need for friendship and the health benefits of having good friends. Like our dogs, our friends can help extend our life expectancy and reduce heart disease. I read in the Bible that God called Abraham His friend and ever since then I knew I wanted to be a friend of God!

And so it happened just as the Scriptures say:
'Abraham believed God, and God counted him as
righteous because of his faith.' He was even called
the friend of God.

JAMES 2:23 NLT

Just as Abraham was God's friend, we can be God's friends too! Our friendship with God is the center and life source of the overall health and well-being we seek. God provides human friends and four-legged furry friends that support us as well. He built into them the ability to generate physiological responses (hormones) in our bodies that support peace and happiness. Imagine that!

God created us to be hope givers to those around us, even our pets! Consider these things as you choose your friends. They truly are a blessing in more ways than one.

· ·

Dear Heavenly Father, thank You for being a relational God. I am so grateful that I am in relationship with You through Jesus. I am also thankful that being in relationship with others is beneficial to me on many levels. I will be a blessing to others as they bless me. In Jesus' name I pray, amen.

Time to Paws...

Today I will focus on being grateful for my friendships and also the health benefits I receive by being the human to my dog. What a great trade-off!

_____

_____

_____

_____

_____

_____

_____

_____

_____

_____

_____

_____

_____

_____

_____

_____

A Sweet Fragrance

My dog has the cutest little nose and is always smelling and inhaling everything and everyone. When he comes up to a stranger, he starts sniffing away. When he gets near another dog, his snout goes into full-blown detect mode!

I find it so fascinating that dogs can smell over a thousand times better than their humans. I have a very keen sense of smell myself, but I guess it truly pales in comparison to the sharp sense of smell my canine has. God designed humans with over five million olfactory receptors, which is what gives us our sense of smell. Did you know that we are even able to detect over one thousand different odors? In comparison, God designed dogs to have over 200 million olfactory receptors. Amazingly, dogs can smell things buried as deep as 40 feet underground! We are all indeed fearfully and wonderfully made by our Creator.

It is very fascinating to read about the different smells that dogs love and those they despise. They tend to run far from all citrus smells. That is handy information for anyone who may want to house train their pet. A dog will not mark an area where the odor is offensive to them. That's kind of funny that humans like citrus potpourri and dogs like smelly socks and shoes.

Dogs smell so acutely and identify us because we each emit a different smell. Just like our fingerprints are uniquely ours, we also carry a scent that is "paws down" our own. I believe we leave a spiritual smell as well. I often wonder what kind of scent trail I leave. Do I leave a sweet fragrance of love with others? Do I leave behind a vapor trail of value that lingers and permeates the atmosphere long after I'm gone? I hope I leave a fresh fragrance of kindness with people.

The Bible says we are the pleasing aroma of Christ Jesus. That is the fragrance we are to be to all the world and how the Lord God Himself sees us.

For we are to God the pleasing aroma of Christ
among those who are being saved and those who are
perishing.

2 CORINTHIANS 2:15

We have all been around some unpleasant smells before, and we have been around some mephitic people as well. Sometimes we can blame those smells on the dog, but other times we just have to own up to them ourselves. The pungent smell of regrets and mistakes has plagued many of us at one time or another.

Some people we encountered may have smelled of brokenness or addiction. Some may have reeked of drugs or alcohol. Others may have had the stench of bitterness, abuse, or condemnation on them. Regardless of the scent others release, we need to love people right where they are. That's what Jesus does—He loves us in all our mess and stink. Every day we have the opportunity to be the perfume of life to those caught in a downward spiral. We can be a sweet and refreshing aroma to the world in the way we conduct ourselves, in the manner in which we value and respect others, in the words we say, as well as in those we don't speak. I just pray that I never again reek of judgment or have the foul stench of pride.

The Bride of Christ is to be a fresh aroma. When other people are around us, they should have the exquisite scent of a loving Father linger in the atmosphere long after we have left their presence. The Bible says that we are to live a life filled with love, just like Jesus did. The way He offered Himself as a sacrifice was a pleasing fragrance to God.

Let's develop this discipline and strive to perfect it for the rest of our lives. Let's leave others better than we found them. Make deposits of blessings, kind words, and good deeds to everyone you encounter. Be a fresh aroma and pleasing fragrance of Christ Jesus to all whom you encounter.

Who knows, maybe you carry the aura of beauty and love that someone needs that will change the entire trajectory of their life! I pray it is so!

Dear Heavenly Father, I pray for a sensitive nose and a sensitive heart for others as I encounter them each day. May I always leave a fragrant offering of kindness, compassion, and love to everyone with whom I come in contact. Please show me who I can take a moment to be good to each day. In Jesus' name I pray, amen.

Time to Paws...

Today I will be mindful of being a sweet and pleasant aroma for others. I will be intentional on leaving a vapor trail of value in each person and be the perfume of life to all.

_____

_____

_____

_____

_____

_____

_____

_____

_____

_____

_____

_____

_____

_____

Waiting at the Door

If I am gone for any measure of time, it never fails that when I return home, my dog is standing at the back door waiting for me to open it. If I happen to be in my bedroom and I close my door, it isn't long before I see a shadow under the crack of the door. My precious pooch is waiting right on the other side of that door for me to open it and invite him in. He waits so patiently on the other side of that door for his invitation, and he is thrilled when I invite him in.

In very much the same way, we have a Savior knocking on the door of our heart just waiting for us to open it and invite Him in. Jesus is such a gentleman that He does not bust the door down or force His way in. He knocks and then waits for us to open the door.

Here I am! I stand at the door and knock. If anyone
hears My voice and opens the door, I will come in and
eat with that person, and they with Me.

REVELATION 3:20

When I searched as to why dogs sit by the door, I found out that it is simply because they missed you. They heard you were coming and wanted to be the first to greet you. To be honest, that makes me tear up a little bit because I can just picture Jesus at the door of your heart, knowing that He loves and misses you so much. He wants to be in relationship with you and is just waiting for you to respond.

As happy as Arrow is when I let him in my room, Jesus is more excited when you open your heart to receive His love, His mercy, and His forgiveness. He wants to be the very first one to greet you when you do open that door and invite Him in to be the Lord of your life. Jesus is standing at the door of your heart this very moment waiting for you to respond to His invitation to have a personal relationship with Him.

What does that mean when you do respond and open your heart and give your life to Jesus? First, you must believe that Jesus is the Son of God. You believe that He died on the cross for all your sins and mistakes, and you repent. Repent just means to turn around. You do an "about-face" from doing life your way, and you begin to follow Jesus. You put your faith and trust in Him. You believe in Him. The job of the believer is easy; it is to believe.

The moment you invite Jesus in, the Bible says your name is written in a big book called the Lamb's Book of Life. The angels in Heaven rejoice as one more comes to the Family of God. Just as our dogs are always so incredibly happy to see us back at home, all of Heaven is having a party as one more son or daughter returns home. You have been missed because you are loved and cherished. Your pet is overjoyed to have you back home. Similarly, Jesus is overjoyed to have you back home with Him for all eternity.

I am so thankful that I opened the door of my heart when I heard Jesus knocking. Be very still and quiet for a moment. Do you hear Him knocking? Will you please let Him into your heart?

If you are ready to open your heart to Jesus, please turn to page 238 for the salvation prayer.

. . . .

Dear Heavenly Father, thank You for knocking and waiting patiently at the door of my heart. I open up the door of my life to Jesus and invite Him in. I may not understand everything right now, but I do know that You love me and want to be in relationship with me. I accept that. I turn from my ways to follow Jesus and believe in Him. Thank You for thinking of everything and making it so easy for me to believe and receive. Please forgive all of my sins and wash me clean. In Jesus' name I pray, amen.

Time to Paws...

Today I will be mindful that Jesus is in my heart to stay. Every time I come home and see my four-legged family member waiting for me, I will think about how happy the Lord is that I am home as His family member.

_____

_____

_____

_____

_____

_____

_____

_____

_____

_____

_____

_____

_____

Salvation Prayer

Romans 10:9-10 says, "If you declare with your mouth, 'Jesus is Lord,' and believe in your heart that God raised Him from the dead, you will be saved."

. . . .

Dear Heavenly Father, thank You for loving me. Thank You for giving me the greatest gift I could ever receive—Your Son, Jesus. I believe that Jesus died on the cross for my sins and rose again to live forever. Please forgive me of all my sins and come into my heart to be my Lord and my Savior. I put You on the throne of my life. I believe and receive that all my sins are forgiven, and You remember them no more. My faith and Your amazing grace have saved me. Thank You, Lord! In Jesus' name I pray, amen.

If you just prayed that prayer and asked Jesus into your heart, let me be the first to congratulate you, welcome you into the Family of God, and tell you how happy I am for you! As a matter of fact, the Bible says that angels rejoice over one soul that repents and turns toward God. Please visit www.MyDogCanPreach.com and let me know about your decision. I would be honored to hear from you and I'd like to send you a gift to support you on your new journey of faith.

Prayers for Your Pet

When Your New Pet Joins the Family:

Dear Heavenly Father,

You are the Creator of all life and how grateful I am that You created my new pet _____. Please let him know how loved he is as he transitions to find his place in my family. Please help me to make the necessary adjustments to make sure he is secure and well cared for. I ask for Your love to overflow from me so that I can love him and comfort him. Thank You, Father, for the gift of my four-legged family member! I know he will bring me many years of joy and companionship. Help me to be a good family member to him as well. Help me to be patient with him as he gets potty trained or is teething. Help me to comfort him when he is sad or not feeling well. More than anything, help me live up to be the person that he thinks I am. I thank You.

In Jesus' Name I pray, amen.

When Your Pet is Lost:

Dear Heavenly Father,

Even as Your watchful eye is upon me, I ask that You keep Your watchful eye upon my pet. Please keep him safe from all harm and temptation. Please protect him and shelter him as You do all of Your creation. Father, I ask that You allow a caring person to find him and then contact me immediately so that we can be reunited. Please help him to be brave and help me to be brave too. I declare in the name of Jesus that no harm will come near my beloved pet. I declare that he will be found, and we will be together again very soon.

In Jesus' Name I pray, amen.

Prayer of Thanks and Protection for Your Pet:

Dear Heavenly Father,

I love my pet so much! I thank You for the gift that he is to me and for sending him to live with me. I dedicate him back to You and ask that You always keep him safe from all harm. Protect him all of his days from all sickness and disease. I believe and declare in the name of Jesus that You will give him a long and healthy life. Let me be a blessing to him even as he is to me. Let me learn from him about unconditional love and discover how much You love me. I thank You for the great gift of my dog and for the greater gift of Your Son, Jesus.

In Jesus' Name I pray, amen.

When Your Pet is Ill:

Dear Heavenly Father,

I come before You in the powerful name of Jesus giving You great thanks because You hear my prayer. I am so grateful that we can bring all of our cares to You because You care so much for me. I lift up my pet _____ and ask that You would touch him and heal him. Your Word tells us that not one sparrow falls to the ground without You being fully aware of it, so I know you care for the animals. Of course, You do! You created every living thing. Please take this sickness from my pet. I know that You specialize in healing the sick and my beloved pet is no different. The same stripes that Jesus took for my healing, I apply to my pet's life. Come and touch him, Lord. Heal him of all sickness and disease. Comfort him as only You can, and I ask that the manifestation of his healing be accelerated in the name of Jesus. You are full of compassion for Your creation. Please show Your unending compassion and mercy right now for _____. I will tell everyone that You are the One who healed him. I praise You and I thank You ahead of time.

In Jesus' name I pray, amen.

When Your Pet Passes:

Dear Heavenly Father,

My heart is so very heavy and sad at the passing of my precious _____. I thank You for creating _____ and choosing me as his parent. I know You are the Creator of every living thing and I know You love Your creation. I am so grateful to know that I will see my be-loved _____in Heaven. Please hug him for me. Thank You, God, for receiving him into Your Kingdom. Thank You for all of the love he brought me for all these years. I grieve hard because I love hard. I am so thank-ful that I can grieve with Jesus who always comforts and consoles me. Please give me the strength and the courage to move forward without my beloved dog. He will be so missed. Please Lord, heal my broken heart. Let me feel Your presence like never before and be comforted.

In Jesus' Name I pray, amen.

Acknowledgments

Writing this book was so much fun and more enjoyable than I ever imagined. When you're surrounded by incredible people cheering you on, it makes all of life better. I know that I am surrounded with the very best.

Thank you to my husband Mills and our son Rob who are the loves of my life and my joy in each day. Mills, thank you for your steadfast love, unwavering support, and encouragement each and every day for the past 28 years. No matter what I endeavor to do, you back me 100%! I am so grateful to Jesus for choosing you for me. I love you. Rob, you always add so much light and laughter to my days. You inspire me to rise higher and challenge me to dig deeper. You make me a better Christian. I am especially proud of the man you have become, and eternally grateful God chose me to be your mom! I love you so much, son!

To my Dad—You and mom raised all eleven of us children to love the Lord and to love one another. So many of the valuable lessons I learned in life was because you instilled in each of us the importance of integrity, honesty, and respect. I am so very thankful that God allowed me to be the daughter of Vic and Virginia Schneider. I love you, Dad!

To My Awesome Siblings—I get emotional thinking about all the love I have for you. The Schneider Family loves big and we love with all that we have. Stephen, you're a great big brother and have always set a good example for us to follow.

Thanks for letting me hang with you and Donna on weekends while I was in college. Valerie, thank you for teaching me how to encourage others and to be bold in doing so. Victoria, you spoke something into my life that evening in Colorado that opened my eyes and my heart to something I had never imagined. Wow! Thank you. Shavonn, thank you for all of the love, the encouragement, the ideas, the wisdom, prayers and support, and the phone calls, etc. I am a much better person because of you! My beloved brother Mark, you are in my prayers every single day and night. I love you. Sweet Annie, thank you for doing life with me and for being so adorable that people always gave us free stuff. What fun memories we have! Chris, my Silver Fox, you are still my favorite dance partner! Fred, you took such great care of Scout when he was a brand-new puppy. "Bear" would have been a great name too! I love you and I miss you. Jennifer, thank you for inspiring me so many years ago to have a more intimate walk with Jesus. Victor, thank you for being the other bookend to our family and for always being such a gentle, yet strong support. To all of my extended family, I love and appreciate you all!

To Mom Worsham—I am so grateful to you for raising such an amazing son that I get to call my husband. Thank you for always loving me and welcoming me into your family. I love you so much, mom.

To Les and Leslie Worsham—I am so thankful to have you as my family and my friends. You are both great people who have raised four wonderful children. I love all of you so much! Leslie, thank you for loving Rob as your own and for being so good to him. Now let's write your book!

To Beverly and Jae Moore—I have so much gratitude and love in my heart for you both. You accepted me into your family and trusted me with your children. You have always been there for me and I am so grateful to God for you! Beverly, thank you for standing beside me at my wedding. Jae, I will never forget you baptizing my newborn son with your tears as you held him and prayed over him. Thank you both for all that you have done for me and meant to me the past 30 years. Thank you especially for the amazing opportunity you blessed me with to write this book. Your friendship is a great gift to me, and I love you both more than I could ever adequately express.

To Victoria and Joel Osteen—Thank you for all the love, prayers, inspiration, and wisdom you have instilled in me the past 15 years. I have learned and grown so much under your teaching and leadership. Thank you for welcoming me into your family and for entrusting your children to me. Jonathan and Alexandra, I love you and am so very proud of you. My precious Victoria, thank you for the beautiful foreword you wrote for this book. You have always given me your best. I remember the time I was in Reno and you stayed on the phone praying with me throughout the night when I was so scared and felt so alone. I will never forget that. Thank you for all of your steadfast love, great advice, and multitude of prayers throughout the years. I love you all with all my heart.

To Joanna and Chris Boyer —I could never have done this without you nor would I have wanted to. Thank you for making this entire process so much fun. You are such a joy to work with and a master at your craft!

To Brandon Bain at Because Marketing—this is the second project we have worked on together. You are a master at your skill. Thank you for using your gifts and talents to bless others and honor the Lord.

To Carolyn Laskie, my BFSTG—From the time you were my teacher in high school up to this very day, I thank you for all your help and encouragement! You are still a great teacher and friend!

I have so many friends I want to thank, but this book would be twice as long if I named them one at a time. My Tribe knows who they are! I love you all from the bottom of my heart!! I thank all of my friends who supported this project and cheered me on. My beloved teachers and mentors, I thank you for all that you have sown into my life. I am so grateful for you. I thank my precious friends in the GIFT Class. I love you so much! To all of my Lakewood Church Family, thank you!

Scout and Arrow—what a dynamic duo. You have both brought great love and joy to our family. Thank you for showing me so much of the Lord's unconditional love.

I am saving the BEST for last because HE saved me! *I thank my Lord and Savior Jesus Christ*—for loving me, redeeming me, and reconciling me back to my Heavenly Father. Jesus, You are my life and breath and the only reason I can love others with all abandon. I hope You enjoy this book and I pray that Heaven gets a lot more crowded because of it. Thank You for giving me and trusting me with this fun assignment!

Special Thanks

I want to thank these very special family members and friends who have supported me and this book with their overwhelming kindness, love, prayers, and generosity.

Shavonn and Marvin Allensworth

Susan Butler

Necie and Audie Gray

Beverly and Jae Moore

Robert Ortiz III

Victoria and Joel Osteen

Kaleena Rallis

Paul Rallis

Jennifer Schneider

Vic Schneider

Oraios Ward